Published by

The Centre for Learning and Teaching in Art and Design (*cltad*)

65, Davies Street

London

W1K 5DA

Reflections on learning and teaching in fashion education

Annual Conference 2005

International Foundation of Fashion Technology Institutes (IFFTI)

ISBN 0-9541439-4-9

British Library Cataloguing-in-Publication Data.

A catalogue record for this book is available from the British Library.

Designed by Meg Richardson and Felix Lam

Printed in Great Britain by

Oxonian Rewley Press Ltd

Oxford

Printed on paper produced from sustainable forests.

Reflections on learning and teaching in fashion education

Contents

Preface

Reflections on learning and teaching in fashion education

This publication is the outcome of an initiative supported by the International Foundation of Fashion Technology Institutes (IFFTI) to promote debate about approaches to learning and teaching in fashion education and to share innovation and emerging best practice amongst the member institutions. IFFTI was founded with the specific purpose of creating a global network of institutions, which could work together to advance education for fashion design, technology and business, and this initiative provided an exciting opportunity for faculty to reflect on their practices as educators and present those reflections at the annual conference held at the National Institute of Fashion Technology in New Delhi in 2004.

Managing the initiative has been an enlightening project in itself, highlighting the contextual, and indeed contested, nature of what " innovation" and "good" or "best" practice might mean to different groups of fashion educators around the world. Although the member institutions are all recognised nationally and internationally as leaders in the field of fashion education, they have developed within quite different cultural, political and educational contexts and their size and scope varies considerably. The papers presented at the conference reflected this diversity not only in their subject matter but also in the ways that scholarly and research activities in pedagogy are approached. The six papers published in this slim volume have been chosen to celebrate this diversity and give a flavour of the ways in which fashion and fashion education is perceived in different parts of the world and in different kinds of institution. For this reason each of the contributors have been asked to contextualise their contribution with a brief description of the institution in which they work.

Garcia, Castilho and Garrido focus on fashion as a collaborative discourse, a means of communicating and sharing meanings. Their paper examines the contribution of the virtual learning environment and net-based resources to fashion education and to the Brazilian fashion industry. For both Panwar, and for Li Shu Wan, fashion is a business and fashion education is about preparing students for specific roles within the fashion business. Both offer alternatives to what they see as "traditional" teaching methods: Panwar examines the value of learning through the " live retail method of education" and Li Shu Wan describes the benefits of problem-based learning and a student centred approach. For Piotraut, fashion is a necessary compromise between the world of inspiration and creativity, and that of industry and trade. She argues that providing opportunities for students on postgraduate programmes in design and in management can improve their understanding of each other's disciplines, ways of thinking and working and could contribute to the development of a constructive dialogue between designers and managers in the industry. Sukino and Ikeda represent fashion design as a process based on information analysis, and their paper addresses the need to integrate digital applications into the curriculum in order to meet the demand for customised clothing. For Shreeve and Kelly working in the context UK educational policy, fashion design is an individual creative endeavour, a practice- and skill- based activity, and they examine the importance of enabling students to develop communication skills specific to the design and realisation process.

Finally we would like to thank Dr D.K Batra, Professor Trevor Little, Dr Pauline Terreshorst and Karen Webster for acting as the editorial board and to Jeni Bougourd, Dr Linda Drew, Tim Jackson, and David Rowsell for their comments.

Elizabeth Rouse
Chair of the IFFTI Initiatives Committee
Pro Rector Academic Development and Quality
University of the Arts London

Sue Parkinson Bailey
Head of Learning and Teaching, Faculty of Art and Design
Manchester Metropolitan University

The influence of virtual learning communities on fashion online teaching experience

Carol Garcia, Kathia Castilho and Sérgio Garrido
Anhembi Morumbi University, São Paulo, Brazil

When an individual faces his or her drawers and hangers in order to make a choice between this or that item of clothing, that individual is making a statement which will echo not only through the day, but also through his or her life. One might add, as we did in previous articles (Garcia, 2002a, p. 34; 2002b, p. 21), that the individual is 'writing' his or her own sentences on everyday scenes, allowing what Bystrina (1995, p. 16) calls 'second reality'[1] to interfere on the visible layers of his/her self. Therefore, it is evident that fashion includes much more than clothes: it is what people do to their bodies to maintain, create or change their appearances so that they can sustain a dialogue with others[2] and establish bonds, arguably fraternal ones[3].

If we take into account Pross (1980) and Baitello (1999) – studies recognising that the body is the first of all media – we might say that fashion could be viewed as a secondary medium, in the same way as photographs and letters are considered. This is due to the fact that it recovers writing functions in terms of registering the way of life in certain times and civilisations. Overlaying the body and its unique

---

[1] According to Bystrina, the first reality would be linked to biological and physical aspects of an individual, relating itself to technique, while the second reality would be the one generated from imagination and fueled by creativity. 'The second reality is a game, but also a dream or a vision. The plurality and diversity of the second reality is much bigger than the ones on the first reality levels. In fact, they are additions to the first reality' (Bystrina, 1995, p.16).

[2] Fashion as a group attachment element has been the focus of studies by numerous researchers, being Polhemus (1994) one of the most acclaimed with books such as *Street Style* (London: Thames & Hudson). For further reference on such subject in Brazilian fashion environment, we suggest the reading of a series of essays by regional fashion journalists, which were edited by Castilho and Garcia (2001) in *Moda Brasil: Fragmentos de um Vestir Tropical* (São Paulo: Anhembi Morumbi Publishers).

[3] Emotional bonds in human communication are displayed as a system presented by Baitello (1999) in many lectures; some of which became essays organised in *O animal que parou os relógios* (São Paulo, Annablume).

gestures, fashion orchestrates and improves human communication skills, functioning as a language. It links individuals in groups who share preferences and goals, regardless of other trends that might occur simultaneously. As a matter of fact, this imagistic writing form survives the fragility of bones and muscles, going beyond time and space. As Villaça (2002, p.40) explains, when commenting on different interaction possibilities distinguished by Thompson, 'on mediated interactions, such as letters and phone conversations, it is a technical mean (paper, electric lines, electromagnetic waves etc.) that makes possible the transmission of information and symbolic contents to individuals living in different spatial and temporal contexts'. Therefore, as a secondary medium, fashion allows humankind to dive into its past and absorb its own evolution, defying death and oblivion.

Accepting the premise that to communicate is to create and to maintain bonds among people, we firmly believe that fashion proves its value by extending an invisible net. As Baitello (2000) puts it, 'the [fashion] image becomes a line to create writing as well as the thread is woven to originate surfaces, to make cloths, to constitute nets'. Nevertheless, if fashion survives the bodies it covers by spreading itself through emotional webs, its rhythm is not biological and can be much more accelerated than first thought by either Pross or Baitello in their early studies. Researches conducted by Valli et al. (2003) figured out that the high speed at which fashion language evolves through new trends spread by mass media results in a multiplication of 'prêt-a-porter images', sometimes doubtfully ethical. Such second-hand images, as far as they produce 'appearance formulas', dislocate themselves into the kingdom of non-communication and become discourse fragments. Mostly borrowed from fashion magazine editorial and advertisement pages (be they printed, electronic or digital), such images are generally framed as a one-way ticket to mass media ready-to-wear illusions. The first reality, with the technique of serial reproduction, predominates and eliminates any trace of the second reality, forcing imagination to pull back. Distant from their original context, they are simply applied as sticking plasters on different subjects. Fashion meaning gets lost in an excess of data and there is no fun left in elaborating and discussing one's appearance. Echoing a chorus, more than offering a personal aesthetic slang, 'it is no longer a game, becoming, at the most, a forced imitation' (Huizinga, 2000, p.10).

Bystrina (1995, p. 15) teaches us that only amusing approaches can interrupt tedious processes in life: 'as an incentive of human activity, entertaining exercise is part of searching for innovation'. In order to maintain its language function and act as a secondary medium, fashion cannot lose its individual accent, or its ability to establish emotional bonds, otherwise it might become artificial and tasteless. So, no matter the risks previously mentioned, we assume that fashion language can be used as a tool 'to deal with the unsafety and uncertainty of contemporary symmetries' (Baitello, 1999, p. 80). Moreover, its natural ability to adhere to and even modify other languages by expanding their meanings would primarily lead to unparalleled opportunities of interaction. If the composition of appearance is an entertaining game – any person may evoke the second reality using fashion language, as we recognised above and before (Garcia, 1999a, p. 42) – therefore it requires other participants, partners and players with whom bonds are established, generating true communication. Why should fashion learning processes be different? We firmly believe they shouldn't. As far as we are concerned, fashion education needs dynamic interaction. And it can be powered by a network of individuals who share the same interests and goals.

If, some years ago, educational processes were seen by individuals as fixed phases that were finished when their careers began, they are currently viewed in the knowledge society as being endless and requiring teamwork. Any individual with minimum access to the Internet and other digital technologies is expected to foresee, project and recycle data on a daily basis, self managing his or her learning processes. However, the excess of inputs might be so intense and confusing that it can appeal to restricted consumption of qualified information instead. These facts lead us to admit that professional survival of knowledge society workers depends upon formal and continued education: the first one for qualification and the second one for updating. Our hypothesis is that human beings would seek educational products with high interaction levels much more than a huge flow of information, so that they could create their own kaleidoscope of learning choices to fulfill both needs. In addition to that, we argue that cyber communities can face those needs capturing fragmented data and offering such information to be processed on behalf of individual knowledge and collective learning. Consequently,

4

the answer might rely on new technologies applied towards group knowledge building. In this sense, the cyberspace can serve as a compass to rethink and organise fashion education as long as it is thought of as an emotional bond net, a surface where links flourish through lifelong learning processes.

This is especially true if we think of the vastness of Brazilian territory not only as geographic matter. Its people express, in everyday habits, diversities and affinities that make the country an effervescent cultural cauldron (Castilho and Garcia, 2001). When forming a multicultural society, individuals from different ethnic backgrounds reveal various market niches, some of them still little explored. This is due to the fact that national interest in fashion subjects is pretty recent in Brazilian society, despite the importance of the textile chain to local economy[4]. In fact, it was only a decade ago that fashion culture came to life in Brazil thanks to regular events, press coverage and government incentive. However, it was still too attached to the elite for a long period and information was spread only in determined circles of power.

That was when a group of professors from the Fashion Design undergraduate course at Anhembi Morumbi University noticed that teaching based in oral tradition was becoming incompatible with such social transformations and the new rhythm of the Brazilian fashion movement. It was a system in which users were simply 'swallowing' the rare information exposed by the printed press on what was going on, instead of reflecting over the recent facts. In 1995, the group, coordinated by professor Kathia Castilho, PhD., started to look for unusual procedures in which information could be researched and better assembled little by little into new forms of knowledge.

Inexpensive, democratic and flexible, it was the Internet that offered a way for students' researches to be transformed into interactive discussions, moving around themes chosen by themselves. Due to this new technological possibility, concepts of teaching and learning were drastically reviewed and a non-linear net of information about the Brazilian fashion scenery was born one year later: the digital magazine *Moda Brasil* (www.modabrasil.com.br), which relates fashion to behavior, technology, society and the arts[5]. The beginning was incredibly simple: fashion students and professors brought to light their

[4]The Brazilian textile chain is nowadays composed by more than 20,000 companies and offers jobs to 1.4 million workers around the country.

[5]*Moda Brasil* has been producing and analysing up-to-date information on style and fashion issues since 26 August, 1996. At that time Brazil was rediscovering its fashion roots and simultaneously the Internet was starting to make a global difference on spreading fashion news. For instance, it was around those years that Austrian designer Helmut Lang astonished the fashion world when he decided to cancel his (live) show in order to perform a virtual catwalk through his website.

own researches. The mission was to dig for originals that could be traced in Brazilian fashion history. *Moda Brasil* compiled biographies of the most important designers and their production, encouraging students to go deeper in their researches. New researches expanded the *Moda Brasil* database with the creation of an online dictionary of fashion terms, an online textile dictionary, an online library (with a search mechanism that locates titles available off-line in the university's own library), as well as home pages of the best Brazilian young fashion designers, recovering their careers. This rich exchange of information evolved into a garment industry virtual museum, which counts on free participation of the community. Viewed as prospective students themselves, contributors are welcome to send fashion stories and produce articles, always helped by teachers and using the Web as means of communication. Such contributions are selected by subject and displayed in sections to facilitate navigation, taking into account hyperlinks to related subjects. The virtualisation of contents actually does what has always been *Moda Brasil's* educational goal: to recreate, reformat and rewrite fashion contents as well as spread them through the Web.

Such initiatives showed a market niche for online education products: students that wanted a glimpse of the brand new world of Brazilian fashion in order to decide on a career in the area. Moved by the quick development of new information technologies, a first experience of an online course totally through the Web was launched, focused on basic notions of fashion for first-year students. The course, entitled 'Fashion Universe'[6], was launched in 1997 and offered primitive forms of interaction mediated by a teacher. Interaction was constituted mainly by discussion lists and exercises sent to the tutor through the Web. It was offered free of charge for one year so that it could be used as research material for new courses and the reworking of methodology. Through these efforts, the efficiency of such experience was largely adapted and new tools emerged. All of these tools together were able to be converged into a thematic network structure that students put together themselves in accordance with their own individual requirements.

At that time, the content published on the *Moda Brasil* website, beyond being developed by teachers and students altogether, was accessed by

[6]Contents were developed by professor Dario Caldas (1999), whose experience was later transposed to the book *Universe of Fashion - online course* (São Paulo, Anhembi Morumbi Publishers).

6

numerous education institutions in Latin America and revealed itself as an important source of fashion information. Consequently, in 1998, *Moda Brasil* was invited to become a content partner of Online Universe Group (www.uol.com.br), a joint venture between *Folha de São Paulo,* one of Brazil's most influence newspapers, and Abril Cultural, a major national magazine publisher. One year later, the website was also acclaimed by fashion researchers nationwide to be an ethical model of fashion information debate through the building of a virtual knowledge community, for it invited fashion journalists to sign columns on themes that weren't commonly addressed in their magazines of origin, mostly relating fashion to art, consumption and ethical issues. This informal digital magazine, assembled almost intuitively, was the first step the university took to establish a formal learning structure. The inputs from various specialists in relation to everyday attempts of technical improvement and software development made the thought of a formal online course more tangible. In other words, one can say that the *Moda Brasil* experience might be seen as a seed of the regular digital courses established a few years later, all of which follow Brazilian educational authorities' requirements.

In 1999, the reduced cost of computers and other equipment allowed growing access to new information technology. At that time, 9% of the urban population already had some means of accessing the Web in Brazil. In São Paulo, 53% of computers were connected and the users' profile revealed that 68% were between 15 and 29 years old. In search of a way to appropriate new communication tools, Anhembi Morumbi University ignited the process by stimulating technological development for educational purposes. It launched in that year its first graduate online course on Fashion and Communication[7]. On the reverse of the website initiative, this graduate course had a formal structure including weekly lessons and scheduled activities that involved all people relating to the course: students, teachers, web experts, technicians. Innovations such as live interaction and the visualisation of course contents combined with freedom from fixed schedules. Teaching time and location approached the goal of a learning path customised to each student. These online classes are considered customised because each student can choose the best time to study, for content is offered online during the whole week. The class content can be studied in different login sessions. It can also be printed and taken

[7]From mere 32 paid enrollments to the graduate specialisation course in August 1999 numbers jumped to 173 registered students in August 2001 (Castilho and Garcia, 2003, p. 141) and 240 in February 2004.

by the student to be read elsewhere off-line. The way to start a lesson is also very flexible. It can be studied either by reading texts, by navigating through suggested sites or by sharing comments on the subject in digital forum sessions and chats, which are always analysed and commented on by the instructor. Therefore the learning process depends a lot on the student's own timetable, self discipline and preferences.

In order to succeed, the teacher role is to be an agent of stimulus and constant incentive for the student to go further in his or her questions, always customising the attention to each participant. Coordination reinforces this attitude, creating an interface for virtual meetings with professionals, other researchers and institutions that promote common knowledge, so that students are in touch with the real world full-time. A support team helps solve technical doubts as soon as they appear; organising the student agenda and the online registry offers help on academic bureaucratic matters.

Two words were definitely settled as basic pillars of this virtual foundation: 'friendly' and 'interactive'. The relationship among teachers, students and new technologies is sometimes constricted by technical difficulties that can challenge new users. That is why both design and contents should be 'friendly' to navigate and simply organised, to provide easy access at various levels of competence, which certainly helps towards the exploration of new forms of study and discussion.It is considered interactive because distance learning infers discipline and time organisation, as well as motivation. The student's fascination is awakened at the moment when he or she becomes the subject rather than the object of this communication. When students physically enter the classroom, they will meet colleagues with the same goals and a teacher to discuss their doubts. However, in the online learning community, they must interact with people from different places, whose only links are the language – Portuguese – and the subject of study – Fashion. That is why each course should be customised, from contents presentation to the design and navigation system. Professors must feel virtual environments to be their own classroom so that students might assimilate the growing disappearance of time and space gaps as a plus, not at all as an inconvenience. In this sense, the teacher is also an apprentice, because it is his or her task to

8

look for online sources of interesting activities that can be adapted to class purposes.

All things considered, *Moda Brasil* is the perfect medium in which to publish student's researches developed during the course. The website took the role of spreading students' works through the Web and assembling a network. Taking into account constant inputs from these students spread nationwide, *Moda Brasil* made a difference by shortening distances. For instance, people who shared lifestyle codes could reach their favourite brands through students' researches published on the Web, disregarding direct official press mediation in fashion news diffusion. From that point on, scholars were joined by fashion journalists and professionals from related fields (sociologists, anthropologists, costume designers, semanticists, historians, textile experts and marketing advisors) whose collaboration activated fresh information on up-to-date subjects. Nowadays, these correspondents, located in Brazil's most important cities as well as in fashion meccas such as Paris, London and New York, recreate fashion news in singular points of view and provide new perspectives. They provide information about an emerging generation of young designers, regional and major fashion events, working in close interaction with teachers and regular students. During these occasions, professors conduct forums from the catwalks in Brazil and abroad toward specific fashion subjects, most of them suggested by the 40,000 readers that subscribed to *Moda Brasil* e-mail list and weekly free newsletter. On certain occasions, such forums even had sponsors[8], companies willing to extend their own market researches in the cyberspace with a qualified target. For example, that was the case with beauty company L'Oreal, which analysed users' comments on best opinion leaders for beauty products advertisement campaigns. Among the partners, there were companies such as Swarovski Crystals, Alpargatas and Columbia Pictures.

Formal and informal studies converge. The abovementioned and other researches conducted by the *Moda Brasil* e-team started to be presented on the every first Friday of each month at a series of free conferences offered at the Anhembi Morumbi Fashion and Design campus in order to allow 'cyber colleagues' to get to know each other personally. The conference session, named 'Fashion Friday', quickly became a meeting point attended by scholars, designers, industry

[8]In order not to interfere with the website educational purposes, no money was accepted from such companies. The results of forums were exchanged for books or product donations that reverted for participants' own researches. Those donations were based on best opinions given at online forums, which were decided by a committee formed with sponsor company members and university teachers.

representatives and the fashion press, so that autograph sessions, product presentations and discussion panels were included in the programme. But the community interest in exchanging fashion points of view was so overwhelming that it grew to the point of becoming a new online project: fashion journalism Lab Web. Coordinated by professor Carol Garcia, MSc., Lab Web's main purpose is to tutor collaborative works entirely on a Web basis, although it includes free workshop meetings once a week (attendance of which is not mandatory). During these meetings, members get to know Anhembi Morumbi campuses and interact with professionals (editors, reporters, stylists and photographers) from major magazines, websites and newspapers. This is followed by online discussions, events coverage and reports done in team working. In this sense, with intense interaction among professors (live and online), journalists and students, pupils are virtually able to participate and build the contents of *Moda Brasil* magazine. The student role as a relatively passive observer and information consumer changes to a co-builder of knowledge. On the other hand, professionals who participate in the project take joy in assuming a volunteer activity towards citizenship.

Members[9] act as online reporters and each resultant article is edited by a professor and then published in the online magazine, allowing students to receive comments from the general public by e-mail. Publishing their work from their geographic point of view keeps them thinking locally, but extends their action globally. Lab Web offers the chance of training their writing skills and expanding their networking. Members interact with website users that not only read, but also comment and react on their writings. Posted on the Web, these texts also started to attract headhunters, allowing students to be viewed as talents for job opportunities[10]. This led to better quality and diffusion of information on young talents, which made *Moda Brasil* a source of research for companies recruiting workers for jobs in the fashion field. It came out that Lab Web exceeded its original purposes, actually serving as a reference guide for job offers from related industries.

This fact changed the role of professional fashion websites in Brazil, which, from that point on, have been gradually evolving from simple information senders to research conductors, cooperating and facilitating the building of knowledge. Nowadays, around a thousand people

[9]Members of the *Moda Brasil* Lab Web generally come from undergraduate courses on Journalism, Public Relations, Fashion Business and Fashion Design from various schools around the country.

[10]Actually, *Moda Brasil* supplied former Lab Web members as writers, photographers and reporters for online and off-line professional fashion publications nationwide, functioning as a 'quality thermometer' for the market.

[11]According to a survey conducted in May 2000 by Anhembi Morumbi University, 83.07% of *Moda Brasil* users were actually working on their graduate thesis and used the site as a research tool.

10

interact with *Moda Brasil* daily, most of them involved in research projects[11]. Besides, two regional projects took it as a role model and introduced local online fashion magazines: RecModa (www.recmoda.com.br) produced by Faculdade Boa Viagem (Recife, Pernambuco) and Santa Moda (www.santamoda.com.br) organised by Universidade Estadual de Santa Catarina (Florianópolis, Santa Catarina).

The constant and faithful number of readers as well as the interest of other institutions in launching similar projects inspired an off-line initiative towards didactic publications. The first idea was about publishing books and originated from the experience of the website, with selected *Moda Brasil* archive texts that were commonly used in the classroom. *Moda Brasil: Fragmentos de um Vestir Tropical* (Fashion Brasil: Fragments of Tropical Dressing) was launched in 2001, composing a portrait of texts signed by website contributors. Meanwhile, the experience of the online graduate course made professors realise that there was, in fact, a lack of a bibliography in Portuguese. As much as the course contents and format attracted prospective students from all over the country and abroad, they wanted to keep learning after graduating and there weren't many alternatives apart from the website. Therefore, Anhembi Morumbi once again expanded its online experience to the editorial field. In 2004, two courses[12] (Art History on the 20th Century and Fashion History) were adapted to paper and published as books, starting a collection of books named *Fashion and Communication* entirely based upon the online graduate course experience. Each book goes further into subjects presented in online classes, interacting with them and providing a list of films, websites and other books for further individual study. The production of books does not conflict with the ascension of digital learning environments. Oppositely, the concurrent management of new technologies merged with traditional methods of teaching and learning invigorates bonds and does not allow educational institutions to deviate from their primary mission: to inform and, above all, educate.

Digital media allow people to establish non-centered relationships between producers and consumers of knowledge, for they offer closer interaction with no fixed roles determined for such communication agents. That does not mean that they will substitute traditional

[12]More books were included later in the collection, totaling six different publications until May 2005.

classroom appeal: rather, they are more likely to be attached as a means of interaction and production of collective knowledge in a lifelong learning process mediated by the university. This allows the join of first and second realities towards a common goal of true communication among people, defined by strong emotional bonds, which empower a virtual learning community to keep growing despite time and space boundaries. The high credibility and legitimacy level achieved by online and off-line publications, as well as the *Moda Brasil* Lab Web project, inspired the development of a graduate course on Fashion Journalism and Lifestyle. A pioneer in Latin America, the course was settled in 2003. Once again, it targets the community orbiting around *Moda Brasil*: from publicists to Lab Web members who want to expand their activities into classroom scheduled courses. In a live environment, students train how to structure arguments, qualifying them to work as self-managing researchers, while they participate as part of a well-respected online publication. Graduate students act as editors, tutoring Lab Web members and enlarging the previous networking system. This allows them to face everyday challenges in the most efficient ways, for it trains them to manage the use of multiple languages, such as photography and hypermedia design, in proceedings that go beyond writing skills – all of them based on the *Moda Brasil* experience.

According to the market research company Ibope NetRatings (2003a; 2003b), the number of active Internet users in Brazilian homes in August 2003 went up 3.8% compared with July of the same year, reaching 7.537 million of unique users, who navigated around 11 hours and 15 minutes each, overtaking Internet users from major European countries (France, Germany, Italy, UK and Spain). It is interesting to note that the university websites were visited by 30.1% of users, a record for the category that pushes Brazil, in proportional terms, ahead of Europe and the USA[13]. In the following month, Brazilian domestic Internet users spent around 12 hours and 28 minutes each on the Internet, 10.69% superior to the hours navigated in August 2003. Ibope NetRatings (2003a) research shows that teenagers from 12 to 17 years old spent 13 hours and 14 minutes in front of the computer, navigation time that equals seven cinema sessions. Although the big consumption of the Internet in Brazil happens at all age levels, it is a fact that the next generation of university students will consider online tools as a normal part of their daily lives, therefore absolutely part of their

[13]According to this study, access to university websites, in percentage terms, was of 25.9% in Great Britain, 23.1% in the USA and Spain, 22% in Italy and 19.7% in France.

learning activities. This is a clear statement of knowledge demand and of Web potential in the area of education and training which justifies the expansion of *Moda Brasil* and online courses into new educational products.

The Anhembi Morumbi University case study proves that the Internet can be a meeting point where, instead of absorbing second-hand images, individuals can propose new habits, uses and behaviours tutored by teachers, professionals and colleagues. Nowadays, due to the refinement of such technological affairs, one might notice that Anhembi Morumbi University offers two kinds of approaches for students. The first defines traditional pedagogical methods in regions where campuses are physically located and the second is in fact a knowledge universe that lies in the cyberspace: a virtual learning community on fashion issues. This virtual community is generated through the integration of interdisciplinary studies and includes distance learning courses, job opportunities, forums and debates which provide not only useful data to the market in general, but also a rich exchange of information among the participants. It is not, whatsoever, a provocative way of substituting store windows, fashion shows or live classes by computer screens. It is, instead, a way of fully using the most advanced tools of communication technology to emphasise and discuss concepts in the eyes of the consumer, allowing the second reality to interfere in what could be just a frozen mass media process with low interaction levels. As Villaça (2002, p. 41) concludes in her comparison of e-books and printed literature, it all depends on the quality of reception – which, in this case, is very much stimulated in classroom by a 'flesh and bone' teacher – as well as by a good management of technology. We might add to Villaça's comments that online networking produces new manners of learning, due to the dissemination of balanced use of multimedia systems and visual culture, both managing knowledge production. It also inspires the crescent option of lifelong learning on behalf of new work challenges in the Brazilian textile chain.

The Brazilian Textile Industry Association (ABIT) estimates that until 2008 12.3 billion dollars will be invested in machinery, development and acquisition of technology, as well as in professional competence. If statistics keep their speed, workers will have distance learning as an option to enlarge professional horizons. Therefore, due to Brazil's huge territorial distances and the recent introduction of fashion studies as an undergraduate option, universities could extensively profit from online virtual communities at various levels. New ways of organising work, the increasing demand for lifelong learning, a growing service sector (including the preparation of teachers in faraway places) and the emergence of a global market are some of the opportunities that can appeal to the use of such learning methodologies and we dare say that other countries with similar challenges should look attentively to the cyberworld potential to address pedagogical initiatives.

References

Baitello, N. (1999, 2nd ed.), *O animal que parou os relógios* (São Paulo: Annablume)

Baitello, N. (2000 – copyright date) "As imagens que nos devoram". *Sesc Imagem e Violência*. Acessed: 2004, February 16th: www.sescsp.com.br/sesc/hotsites/imagemeviolencia/conferencias.htm

Bystrina, I. (1995), *Tópicos de Semiótica da Cultura* (mimeo) (São Paulo: PUC-SP)

Castilho, K. & Garcia, C. (2001), *Moda Brasil: Fragmentos de um Vestir Tropical* (São Paulo: Editora Anhembi Morumbi)

Castilho, K. & Garcia, C. (2003) "Informatica: um nuovo approcio allo studio della moda attraverso comunità di apprendimento virtuali" in Valli, B.; Barzini, B.; Calefato, P. (eds). *Discipline della moda: L'etica dell'apparenza*. Liguori Editore, Napoli

Garcia, C. (2002), 'Moda e comunicação: o jogo da aparência como raiz cultural', *Nexos*, VI, 9, 2nd semester, pp. 33–48 (São Paulo: Editora Anhembi Morumbi)

Garcia, C. (2002) "Corpo, moda, mídia e mercado: radiografia de uma relação visceral" in Castilho, K.; Galvão, D. (eds). *A moda do corpo, o corpo da moda*. Editora Esfera, São Paulo

Huizinga, J. (2000, 4th ed.), *Homo Ludens* (São Paulo: Editora Perspectiva)

Ibope NetRatings (2003 – October, last update), 'IBOPE eRatings: Internautas brasileiros quebram mais um recorde de navegação', *Ibope e-Ratings*, online (accessed December 2003) at: www.ibope.com.br/eratings/ogrupo/empresa/eratings/index.htm

14

Ibope NetRatings. (2003 - September, last update). "Ibope eRatings: brasileiros batem recorde no acesso aos sites universitários". *Ibope e-Ratings.*Acessed: 2003, December, 08: http://www.ibope.com.br/eratings/ogrupo/empresa/eratings/index.htm

Pross, H. (1980), *Estructura simbólica del poder* (Barcelona: G. Gilli)

Silva, R. (2003), *A moda nos sites jornalísticos especializados* (mimeo) (São Paulo: Imes - Centro Universitário Municipal de São Caetano do Sul)

Valli, B., Barzini, B. & Calefato, P. (eds.) (2003), *Discipline della moda: L'etica dell'apparenza* (Napoli: Liguori Editore)

Villaça, N. (2002), *Impresso ou eletrônico? Um trajeto de leitura* (Rio de Janeiro: Mauad)

Biographical notes

Carol Garcia is the founder and research director of Modus – Marketing & Semiotics, a consultancy company that deals with fashion brands' identity and brand management in South America. A journalist who graduated from Paraná State Federal University (UFPR), she got her Master of Science degree in Communication and Semiotics at São Paulo Catholic University (PUC-SP). As a fashion journalist and researcher she contributes articles and reviews for major Brazilian newspapers as well as art and lifestyle magazines in the areas of fashion creation, communication and consumption. As a professor and head of department she lectures at Anhembi Morumbi University, where she manages the MBA on Fashion Retail and both postgraduate courses on Fashion Journalism & Lifestyle and on Fashion Culture. In the same academic environment Carol has held the position of editor-in-chief at the digital magazine *Moda Brasil* (www.modabrasil.com.br) since 2000. She is also a member of the editorial board of *Fashion Theory* magazine (Brazilian issue) and she volunteers at Latin American Identities – a non-governmental organisation that links designers, industries and schools from Argentina, Chile, Uruguay, Colombia and Brazil for professional and academic exchange. This educational experience led her to produce books such as *Moda Brasil –Fragmentos de um Vestir Tropical* (São Paulo, Brazil: Anhembi Morumbi Publishers, 2001) and *Moda é Comunicação* (São Paulo,

Brazil: Anhembi Morumbi Publishers, 2005). Since then she has travelled around the country and abroad as a lecturer on fashion communication issues.

Kathia Castilho has a doctorate and a master's degree in Communication and Semiotics, courses she attended at São Paulo Catholic University (PUC-SP). She is a specialist in Fashion Design by Academia Internacionale Koefia in Rome, Italy, and has a degree in Social Sciences. She is currently a Textile Technology higher education professor at the University of São Paulo and formerly founded the *Moda Brasil* website at Anhembi Morumbi University, where she coordinates the series of books based on the homonymous online course 'Fashion and Communication'. She is a member of the Fashion Theory magazine publishing board in Brazil and also the author of Fashion and Language (Anhembi Morumbi Publishers, 2004).

Sérgio Garrido is an e-learning consultant and marketing expert with a management degree from Getulio Vargas Foundation, São Paulo. He was formerly the head of department for undergraduate fashion courses at Anhembi Morumbi University, where he currently teaches graduate courses on fashion research issues. He also lectures at prestigious Brazilian universities, such as ESPM (São Paulo), Mackenzie (São Paulo) and Unifacs (Salvador), and contributes on the *Fashion Theory* magazine publishing board in Brazil.

Anhembi Morumbi University was founded in 1970 in the city of São Paulo, Brazil, by a group of friends who shared a passion: advertisement studies. Therefore, its first undergraduate course was totally devoted to the area of social communication. One year later, though, the institution found its true vocation – being inventive – by creating the first higher education course on Tourism in Brazil. This led Anhembi Morumbi founders to put their efforts into creating innovative courses, according to market demand and Brazilian growth needs. Fashion courses started in the early nineties, making a statement of creativity and focus on high educational standards. E-learning was implemented shortly after, involving specialists from various fields in order to create a friendly and trustworthy digital environment for collective learning. Now, Anhembi Morumbi University caters for 27,000 undergraduate and graduate students distributed in four campuses, all of which have access to digital learning tools.

Live fashion retail models as a best practice in fashion education

Dr. Tarun Panwar
National Institute of Fashion Technology, New Delhi, India

Abstract

Fashion education is essentially a form of professional education that caters to the needs of adults who are looking to gain meaningful insights into the world of fashion business. Hence any model that caters to this form of education needs to be 'experiential' in nature. This paper attempts to document and analyse the live retail model in execution as the 'Style Shop' at the Fashion Institute of Technology, New York, which is managed completely by the students of the institute. The live retail model allows the students to put theory into practice. It helps the students to mange a retail shop commercially in a business environment thereby providing a platform for industry, consumer and student interface. The author has additionally analysed similar ventures, like the store operating at the Indian Institute of Management, Bangalore, in order to effectively study the difference in learning students derive from the 'live retail model of education'. He has adopted the 'Grounded Theory' case study method for the same. The paper finally recommends an optional live retail model that can be adapted by fashion institutes to enable them to impart education more effectively.

Overview of literature

The review of the literature survey carried out clearly highlighted the need to understand the emphasis fashion organisations place on practical skills required on the job. It also clearly brought out the need for creating understanding of consumer behaviour, store organisation and merchandising management for adopting a career in fashion retail. The best practices documented so far reveal negligible solutions for creating such understanding.

As Ellen Diamond highlights in her book *The World Of Fashion,* the variety of activities involved in fashion results in jobs that attract people with different backgrounds. In fact, more often than not, what the companies are looking for is an understanding of the broad context in which customers select, buy and use fashion products and services. Fashion is a complex subject, one that fascinates, intrigues and essentially offers challenging, exciting and financially rewarding careers (Stone).

A survey conducted by Howse, Hines and Swinker shows that members of the fashion fraternity rate practical skills, such as buying-criteria planning, critical interpretation of past data, team building and customer-relationship management very high. Results of this study reiterate that, for a successful career in retail, skills such as decision making, negotiating with vendors, merchandise management, understanding needs of customers, resolving frustrating situations at the workplace and knowledge of inventory are of primary importance. Interestingly, the retailers surveyed did not give much consideration to the generic educational criteria which are assimilated in the classroom by means of lectures, case studies, group discussions, seminars, tutorials, presentations, which they felt were only needed to provide the underlying knowledge for executing more efficiently the primary skills listed above. Thus, any attempt at providing fashion education must directly address the need to develop these primary skills and thereby help produce professionals who will assume practical responsibilities rather than produce masters of generic theories, much of which when applied to the problem on hand does not produce the predicted results.

Past research has also shown that successful business ventures require professionals adept at recognising customer needs and desires far enough ahead to have the right products in the right places at the right time and in the right quantities (Zaleznik). This is further established by Patricia B. Seybold's research on 'Getting inside the lives of your customers' in which she stresses the importance in retailing of 'seeing how your products and services fit into the real lives of consumers'.

The medical fraternity currently practices education that directly caters to the needs of the job. We must realise that like the medical profession, fashion too is personal in nature and 'treatment' needs customised operations and services. Hence, akin to medical institutes providing affiliated hospitals in which students can practice, fashion institutes too can operate a retail outlet managed by the students, which will give them an opportunity to apply, question and modify the theories they assimilate in the classroom. Also the pace with which the market changes for fashion businesses hardly allows professionals to try new practices or experiment with existing methodologies. It is this sort of exploratory study that students running their own store can undertake, giving them the opportunity to be innovative.

Another point to be borne in mind is that consumers of fashion education are essentially adults seeking professional education. As elaborated by Nancy Maresh, CEO of Maresh Brainworks, Boulder, Colorado, in her paper 'Breathing life into adult learning', students who are adults seek and perceive patterns, create meanings, integrate sensory experience, and make connections so that they become more proficient at designing and delivering the operations they seek to learn. The 'Left Brain-Right Brain' theory propounded by Dr. Roger Sperry of the University of California also emphasises the importance of differentiating between 'analytic-learning' (left brain) and 'synthesis-learning' (right brain) to enhance adult learning.

While preparing a curriculum for careers as retailers, it is important to incorporate exposure to real-life working scenarios in the education model, which nurtures the skills and competencies needed for the profession. Such education models do exist, but hardly any of them have been analysed and documented for future reference by the education sorority. Prior studies have reported on the shortcomings of the commonly prevalent methods of learning (Goel; Krishnan; Murthy; Rohmetra; Karamanos) but none have documented existing education models that address the shortcomings identified by them.

The literature survey therefore suggested the need to identify and document live retail models that currently exist in premier fashion institutes in order to provide guidelines to other institutes who want to engage in similar efforts.

Methodology

For researching the best practices in fashion education this study started with a literature survey for finding out education practices requirements for pursuing a fashion retail career and developing the case studies for offering the solutions.

The research was carried out with the following objectives:

- developing the case studies of live retail models as a tool for providing hands-on retail experience to the students;
- exploring options and suggestions for benchmarking to be followed by other fashion education institutes to develop live retail models.

The study is primarily exploratory by nature and uses expert interviews, case studies and desk research. The literature survey established the need for conducting the study further by using the case study approach.

In researching the best practice of fashion education, from among the existing models, the 'Grounded Theory' method of case study research (Strauss & Corbin, 1990) has been used. The Grounded Theory approach is a case-oriented perspective that begins with a research situation. Within that situation, the author's task as researcher is to understand what is happening and how the players manage their roles Part and parcel of this approach is a comparative orientation and this paper compares two live fashion retail models as a basis for emphasising a best practice in fashion education Thus, this study is developed inductively from a corpus of data that considers different cases to be wholes, in which the variables interact as a unit to produce certain outcomes assuming that variables interact in complex ways. The cases studied are that of the Style Shop, Fashion Institute of Technology, New York, and Merchandising & Retailing Society, Indian Institute of Management, Bangalore. These cases, similar in many variables but with different outcomes, are compared to see where the key causal differences actually lie (Mills, 1955) and actions that have the same outcome are examined to see which conditions they all have in common, thereby revealing necessary causes. The research tends to focus on making implicit belief systems explicit and at the same time 'discover' or label variables (called categories, concepts and properties) and their interrelationships. It helps identify active variables (causes), keeping in mind the background variables (context), and thereby develops action strategies that can help arrive at the desired results –

effective education to fashion education consumers. Consequences of these action strategies have also been analysed and documented.

In the current scenario, we began with the research situation of understanding live retail models. Within that situation, our task was to understand what is happening at Style Shop/MARS and how students manage their roles. We did this mostly through observation, conversation and interview. After each bout of data collection we noted down the key issues (called 'note-taking' in Grounded Theory parlance). After each bout of data collection, comparison was made to previous bouts of data collection to construct various hypotheses. These hypotheses were refined/modified after each bout of data collection. One advantage of using Grounded Theory is it did does not test hypotheses, but aims to find what accounts for the way students learn at Style Shop/MARS.

Thus, the research results so obtained are aimed at demonstrating their quality not only in the context in which a practical education model is practised, but also in contexts other than this, which is the Indian context. The research exercise also explores adaptations of the existing models to suit these other contexts, so as to provide the readers with circumstance-contingent models that can suit various conditions (Bateson, 1979) and thereby become universally applicable.

The Style Shop, Fashion Institute of Technology, New York

The most successful among the various 'experiential-learning' models of education in fashion institutes across the world is probably the model in execution at the Fashion Institute of Technology (FIT), New York. The institute has developed an 'on-campus boutique' called the Style Shop, which is completely managed by students of the institute.

History

The Style Shop was opened in 1994, as FIT celebrated its 50th anniversary. It is located in the FIT David Dubinsky Student Center. It was opened as the anniversary shop which was to operate only through May 1994, however its success led to the college setting up the Style Shop (it was so named in September 1996), whereby the college created a boutique that was run throughout the year by the FIT faculty, administrators and members of the Merchandising Society, the largest student club on campus. It was an effort aimed at giving the students an idea of what they would be doing as fashion professionals; post their education at FIT.

The initial investment for the store evolved over time, at first the store had to make do with old fixtures purchased at auctions and such other constraints. But now, the shop has generated enough profit to provide new fixtures and facilities for itself.

Institutional support

The store has a floor space of 360 square feet. The institute has donated this space to the students to facilitate the operation of the store. The store is given a stipulated amount at the start of the school year to pay for merchandise, supplies and snacks for meetings and an end-of-the-year party. The institute has also appointed a store operations manager who is on call all the time. Also, a faculty advisor is assigned who is given full responsibility for the store. The administration does not ask for periodic reports. Only if the expenses exceed the budget does a formal requisition has to be placed with the appropriate authorities.

This is the tenth year of its operations and over the years it has proved to be an innovative and enriching way of learning for the students – not just the retail students but for students from the various streams of education offered by FIT. It has proved to be truly representative of the real industry scenario.

Store operations

The students of FIT are allowed to become members of the Merchandising Society by paying an annual fee of $10 and are compulsorily required to dedicate one hour per week to participating in the operation of Style Shop. Depending on the number of students who have opted to be members, various students are allocated specific hours of the day in a week to occupy floor at the shop. On a typical day, the store operates from 9:30 a.m. to 7:00 p.m. except on Fridays when it is open from 9:00 a.m. to 4:00 p.m. Before opening the store, the store operations manager ensures that the merchandise is in order and leaves the designated student in charge. Three students have to be signed up for any hour, so that if someone is sick someone else can take over. At the end of the stipulated hour they hand over the charge of the shop to the student who takes over from them. The process is continued till the end of the day when again the store operations manager scrutinises the logbook to verify that everything is in order. Also, if a student has to leave before his or her replacement shows up, the operations manager opens the door for the next student. A log book is maintained in the store in which the students are required to enter the time they assume charge of the shop and all the sales they make in the one hour that they are managing the store.

The process is seamless in the sense it is very well outlined and efficient. Details involving the store operations are also elucidated exhaustively to the members. Hence the functioning of the store over the years has grown to become systematic and proficient. There are various members of the committee who are appointed in various positions of responsibility in order to ensure the smooth functioning of the shop. However, candidates interested in assuming these positions are required to have prior experience working with the Style Shop. A very comprehensive and systematic procedure of selection is in place that determines which student is designated to which role. The Style Shop addresses various aspects of actual retailing and the students who are part of the Style Shop committee work towards accomplishing the functions that constitute these aspects.

The operation of the store is divided into various tasks. As is required in a real retail outlet, students are involved in inventory management. Students, faculty and alumni are invited to present their merchandise to 'buyers' representing the shop. They will then determine which products are most appropriate to be stocked in the shop. They take decisions on the quantity of the merchandise to be stocked, the selling price of the merchandise and the purchase terms for the merchandise. More often than not, the merchandise is stocked on a consignment basis (80% designer, 20% Style Shop) as this entices students to display their merchandise. With the industry, however, payments are made 30 days after the receipt of the goods in order to exactly replicate the operations of any other store.

These students are also engaged in spotting 'hot trends' on the campus and trying to cater to them through the merchandise the shop sells.

Once the merchandise is in-house, it is sorted and displayed on the basis of various criteria. An item is identified as the 'Hot Item of the Week' and this is prominently displayed in the window facing the High

Street. Decisions are made on mannequin arrangements; merchandise displays and other requirements, which are essentially similar to the visual merchandising exercise that retail outlets engage in. The students try and ensure that the store 'look' is in keeping with the prevailing season of fashion and thus will help increase sales.

All the members of Style Shop who are involved in the operation of the store are given a basic training in customer service, as this is what translates directly into sales. In fact, the entire shop revolves around how effectively the students can serve their clients. Understanding this gives the students an idea of how important it is to understand and satisfy the needs of the customer, especially in an era when customer expectations and needs are changing rapidly. The shop also has periodic customer-motivation programmes, which aim at educating customers about the merchandise and the 'experience' Style Shop sells.

Apart from these obvious functions, the students are also involved in increasing the awareness of the store both within and outside the FIT community. The students also undertake public-relation activities such as press releases and charity events. The college further encourages prospective students and others visiting the campus to stop at the shop. This ensures that customers from outside the college also buy from the store and so the students get a more realistic idea of consumer behaviour.

The shop is financially self-sufficient; operating on a small scale makes it economically viable for the college. However, the financial aspects of the store are managed by the students and this involves financial activities such as everyday sales transactions, purchase terms of merchandise with the students and other such operational activities. This gives the students a fair perspective on the business aspect of retail operations and thus encourages them to plan, make and manage profits. The store realises a profit of 43% annually. Sales from merchandise purchased from the industry account for 33%; an almost equal percentage of sales is derived from merchandise designed and developed by the students and the remaining sales come from merchandise produced with the FIT logo.

The shop tries to simulate a real retail outlet as closely as possible and in keeping with this effort, some students are designated to observe the emerging trends in retail outlets across the world and ensure that Style

Shop is keeping up with the trends as far as possible. These students are encouraged to attend trend shows and showrooms in search of the latest trends. The shop also releases a trend book at the end of each semester. Thus, these students effectively determine the extent to which the Style Shop emulates the real industry scenario.

Apart from following emerging trends in products, Style Shop also sells merchandise that is exclusively designed for it and come with FIT logo designs, similar to private labels that are now becoming so popular. These are marketed as 'Styles', the latest of which are displayed on the website as well. The website is also managed and maintained by the students and they keep it as up-to-date with information regarding Style Shop as possible. The website offers comprehensive information regarding the various teams that help run the shop and also houses information regarding all the activities conducted by the Style Shop with pictures and dates. The website thus acts as the one-stop destination for almost any detail regarding the Style Shop.

Other generic functions, such as marketing, are also provided by the students. The marketing involves conducting advertising campaigns through posters, announcing special promotions and developing pricing strategies. The shop primarily aims to sell trendy and affordable merchandise to students of FIT, who form the majority of the Style Shop clientele. The students responsible for marketing ensure this is done effectively. Despite operating on a small scale, the marketing activities undertaken by the students effectively ensure that they derive full comprehension of the importance of the function.

Though the students essentially manage the store, the college administration appoints a faculty to oversee and, when necessary, to guide the operations of the Style Shop. This professor acts as the nexus between the students and the administration. He or she accompanies students on field visits, helps make final decisions regarding budgetary considerations and ensures that the overall learning students derive from managing the store is in sync with the goals of setting up Style Shop. He is also in constant interaction with the store's operations manager and to some extent the co-manager of the shop. This ensures the proper and appropriate amount of monitoring of the overall effectiveness of the Style Shop by FIT's administration.

To summarise, the Style Shop has proven to be an excellent learning platform for students involved in its operations. It has provided them with an overall understanding of the requirements of a retailing career by addressing the various aspects of retailing such as product design, product selection, product display, customer relations, marketing functions, budgetary activities and industry buying.

Thus, adopting this model of education to impart fashion education is clearly very desirable. However, there are certain factors that are uniquely responsible for the success of Style Shop that may not be universally existent – factors we shall analyse before advocating that it needs to be adopted by all fashion schools.

Why is the Style Shop possible at FIT?

A concept such as Style Shop is successful in an institute such as FIT because of many reasons, some of which are enumerated here. The large student population of FIT ensures that even a dedication of one hour per week by the participating students is sufficient to effectively manage the store. Flexible timings of classroom sessions imply greater scope to participate in such an operation. Also, the large campus – which includes the High Street – offers substantial traffic of customers that the shop can cater to. Finally, the existence of resources, such as the requisite infrastructure, makes Style Shop possible.

The second live retail model is the Merchandising and Retailing Society, an on-campus store that caters to the needs of the students at the Indian Institute of Management, Bangalore. A detailed analysis of the same is provided below.

The Merchandising and Retailing Society, IIM-Bangalore, India
History

Initially known as SACS (Students' Amenities Center Society), MARS was founded on 14 February 2004, in an area of approximately 400 square feet on the Indian Institute of Bangalore campus. The store operates from 8.30 p.m. to 9.15 p.m. only, and the students in the organising team take turns in managing the store.

Institute-industry support:

The institute has not appointed any representative of its own towards operation of the store. The store is run by a core team of ten members.

Of these, three are involved in the purchase operations, two are treasurers and one is responsible for the operations of the store. All the members interact extensively and even their responsibilities and functions are interdependent. The store has a strategic business partner in Himalaya – a well-established ayurvedic products' brand in India. Himalaya has displayed its entire product range in the store and it also makes a monthly payment towards the same in addition to from paying for two hoardings that it displays at the front and the back of the store. The institute has however allocated a stipulated amount per month that the store can utilise.

Merchandise management and store operations

The store is stocking merchandise in its floor space and is now considering the option of displaying it on the Fabmall website, which can be exclusively accessed by the IIM, Bangalore's alumni. The merchandise sold at the shop and its nature of operations is outlined in detail below:

The store has a full range of Himalaya products from cosmetics to medicines, IIMB sweat shirts and tee shirts.

In collaboration with the other student-clubs of the college, the store also offers services such as procurement of tickets/passes for events happening across Bangalore. The store has a tie-up with retail outlets where students get discounts on presentation of their ID cards. It also has tie-ups with various restaurants that allow students special concession rates.

Since the store operates only for an hour per day operations are managed by the ten students who are a part of the core team. The store has its own internal website, which informs students of the various products and the deals that the store is currently offering.

The store generally sells merchandise at a price 5% below MRP. Most of the FMCG products are bought from Metro Cash-n-Carry (every 15 days). Stationery is procured from a local shop near the campus and is subsequently sold at lower prices for the benefit of the students.

The students also make a one-time payment, which is refundable at the time of graduation. This is towards the initial capital required by the store for its operations. The store uses Tally as its billing software.

Hence, the store is taking advantage of the locational inconvenience of the college – outside the city – by providing merchandise used by the students for daily consumption that is not easily available in the vicinity of the college.

A brief comparison of the two models reveals clearly that the FIT model involves wider impartation of knowledge and hands-on experience for the simple reason that it allows a larger number of students to participate in the venture. Also it caters to a larger clientele by allowing anybody to buy from the shop. However, the MARS model is more focused and maybe a good way to kick-start the effort. As operations increase, the model could be revised. Also, in the Indian scenario, which entails rigid class hours, it may be a more convenient model to follow.

The Indian scenario – a representative study of the feasibility of such educational models

Most fashion institutes in India have a curriculum that includes classroom lectures from 9:30 a.m. to 5:30 p.m. This implies that students do not have the requisite time to run a retail store such as the Style Shop. Also fashion is still a developing area of study, hence most institutes, including premier ones such as NIFT, have a limited populace which essentially means fewer individuals to operate such a store and also requires students to dedicate more hours to participating in the endeavour. Besides, space and infrastructure constraints are highly likely, which means that to start a venture of this sort may be physically improbable, if not impossible. Most institutes are moreover located outside the city, which ensures there is no main street that can enhance the customer numbers visiting the store. Also, organised student bodies such as the Merchandising Society are absent in fashion institutes. However, being a niche stream of education, institutes like NIFT have built strong relationships with the corporate entities of the industry. This is a factor that could be leveraged by the institutes when they are considering implementation of live retail models as part of the education offered to students.

Keeping in mind all the above factors and the changing requirements of the Indian industry, a broad outline describing how to go about setting up similar ventures is presented subsequently.

Summary of required action steps to initiate the 'live retail model'

Any fashion institute that hopes to provide an education model that involves establishing a live retail setup will have to plan suitably and take the action steps required to execute the plan. The recommended model for benchmarking is Style Shop of FIT, New York. The author feels that Style Shop is a robust and complete model for establishing such a initiative by the fashion institute. The best practices of Style Shop, well documented in the case study at the beginning of the paper, can be followed for a comprehensive live retail model to be developed by a fashion institute. A brief outline of the required efforts is summarised below.

1 Appoint faculty in charge.

2 Formulate student body (teams) for the retail shop.

3 Select the location.

4 Provide/plan for the initial investment.

5 Plan inventory assortment/buying plans.

6 Institute a website that caters for the shop.

7 Have a launch party.

However, an institute will not always be in the position of undertaking all of the above actions. In such cases, the institute can opt for selective adoption of the model, two of which have been elaborated below.

E-tailing

The institute can set up a website affiliated to its official website that can display merchandise for sale and encourage Web visitors to buy these goods. Such a model has the advantage of not requiring dedicated day-hours from the students. Inventory management is also simplified as there is no requirement of a physical area for the store, thus most of the merchandise stock can be maintained in limited quantities. Financial operations will also be online, the only crucial aspect being order delivery, coordination between collecting purchase requests and merchandise delivery. The functions of visual merchandising are reduced to the display of merchandise on the website. This model also negates the drawback of being located outside the city as it takes the merchandise to the consumer's desktop.

Industry-institute collaborative ventures

Such models are already in practice where a fashion institute has tied up with an corporate entity to run a fashion-related business, thereby enabling the institute to give the students an opportunity to work in a live scenario and, at the same time, giving the company a forum where they can experiment with the settings that run the operations of the outlet (for example the textile mill run at Technological Institute of Textiles and Science, Bhiwani).

Such a store can stock and sell creations by the students and its own merchandise under the same roof. Again the students can spend a stipulated number of hours on the shop floor, managing the operations of the store at no cost to the corporate partner, thus proving to be a win-win situation for both parties.

This model will also augment the industry-institute interaction, apart from giving the students a very realistic picture of the activities of retailing that define the success of a retail organisation. This will ultimately prove to be beneficial for the corporate partner as well, as they can themselves be a part of teaching the students those skills that they look for in students they recruit to occupy positions of responsibility in their organisation. The students can focus on competencies such as analysing and observing business innovations, economically and effectively handle these innovations, identify the shortcomings of these innovations and look for alternatives that can negate these shortcomings. In fact a study by AICTE has shown that these are the skills retailers feel modern students are sorely lacking in.

Conclusion

This paper has documented the case studies of practices followed by education institutes using live fashion retail models to provide a platform for collaborative knowledge creation for three consumers of fashion education – the institute, the student and the industry. In the overview of literature in the study, it clearly comes out that the traditional educational models have been critically evaluated. However, there have been no significant studies conducted that document existing practices that overcome the shortcomings of using traditional models. The paper has developed two case studies, Style Shop at FIT and MARS at IIMB, which clearly provide insights as to how students are involved in management, merchandising, marketing and store operations and how these have provided the students with an overall understanding of the requirements of a retail career. These case studies have shown that hands-on experience and wider impartation of knowledge become a possibility provided the institutions are ready to provide the infrastructure and flexible student learning timings. These models also give the students an understanding of changing consumer expectations and a fair perspective on business aspects of retail operations.

The paper also explores the suggestions/possibilities of establishing such best practices through industry-supported collaborative ventures and e-tailing formats. These suggested models may be revised in terms of the format of the live retail store, but the essence will have to be retained – to focus more on processes rather than on content, minimising the variance between what is taught in class and what is of prime importance to the industry.

It is pertinent to point out that these practices are not only aimed at sustainability in the long run but are aimed at creating learning for the students. The study concludes that providing a live fashion retail environment for the students allows them to put theory into practice. It also enhances confidence in the knowledge acquired through first-hand experience and application. The experiential learning mode in a real-life business environment prepares the students for on-the-job challenges and helps shape their careers.

Acknowledgements

Prof. Jane Werner, Faculty Advisor, Style Shop, FIT, New York.

Ms. Mahalakshmi Rajagopalan, Student, Department of Fashion Management Studies, NIFT, India.

References

Christensen, C. & Raynor, M. (2003), 'Why hard-nosed executives should care about management theory', *Harvard Business Review*, September, pp. 67-74

Diamond, E. & Diamond, J. (2002, 3rd ed.), *The World of Fashion* (New York: Fairchild Publications)

32

Goel, S.K. (2001), 'Need to develop global curriculum in management education', *The Indian Journal of Technical Education*, 24, Oct-Dec, pp. 30-32

Goleman, D. (1998), 'What makes a leader?', *Harvard Business Review*, January, pp. 83-91

Howse, B., Hines, J.D. & Swinker, M.E. (2000), 'Perceived importance of educational criteria to retail buyers', *Journal of Fashion Marketing and Management*, 4, 1, pp. 27-32

Karamanos, A.G. (2003), 'Complexity, identity and the value of knowledge-intensive exchanges', *Journal of Management Studies*, 40, 7 November, pp. 1870-1890

Krishnan, M.A. (2000), 'Development of creativity among professional students', *The Indian Journal of Technical Education*, 23, 1, pp. 44-49

MacLean, P. (1973), *Triune Brain Theory* (National Institute of Mental Health in Bethesda, Maryland)

Maresh, N. (1999, 2nd ed.), 'Breathing life into adult learning', *ASTD Handbook of Training Design and Delivery* (Colorado: McGraw-Hill)

Murthy, S.S. (2002), 'Industry institute interaction', *The Journal of Technical Education*, 25, April-June, pp. 32-37

Rohmetra, N. (2002), 'Personality development – the contribution of professional education', *PARADIGM*, 2, pp. 13-18

Seybold, P.B. (2001), 'Getting inside the lives of your customers', *Harvard Business Review*, May, pp. 81-89

Sperry, R. (1981), *Left Brain-Right Brain Theory* (California University Press)

Stone, E. (1983, 4th ed.), *Fashion Merchandising: An Introduction*, pp. 2-3 (McGraw-Hill)

Zaleznik, A. (2004), 'Managers and leaders: are they different?', Best of Harvard Business Review, January, pp. 75-81

Biographical note

Dr. Tarun Panwar is Associate Professor and Center Coordinator, Fashion Management Studies, National Institute of Fashion Technology, New Delhi, India. He holds a Ph.D. and MBA in the area of marketing. He also studied at Fashion Institute of Technology, New York, in an international fellow exchange programme. He has 15 years experience in teaching, research and industry. His present research interests are in the area of fashion retailing, retail anthropology and innovations in fashion marketing education. He teaches fashion retailing, fashion brand management and fashion marketing strategies to postgraduate students.

He has developed this paper, 'Live fashion retail models as a best practice in fashion education', based on his personal experience of teaching fashion retailing and exposure to institute-run retail stores at NIFT-New Delhi, FIT-New York and IIM-Bangalore. He personally worked at similar stores and interacted intensely with the students to learn the benefits of live retail models.

National Institute of Fashion Technology, New Delhi, was set up in 1986 under the aegis of the Ministry of Textiles, Government of India. It has emerged as the premier institute of design, management and technology, developing professionals to take up leadership positions in fashion business in the emerging global scenario. The institute is a pioneer in envisioning and evolving fashion business education in the country through a network of seven professionally managed centres at New Delhi, Bangalore, Chennai, Gandhinagar, Hyderabad, Kolkata and Mumbai. NIFT has set academic standards and excelled in thought leadership by providing a pool of creative genius and technically competent professionals. The institute serves to provide a common platform for fashion education, research and training & NIFT is also founding member of IFFTI.

Contact details

e-mail: tarunpanwar@niftindia.com, panwar_t@yahoo.com

Managers and designers in the French fashion industry – pooling our talents

Karine Piotraut
Institut Francais de la Mode, Paris, France

Design has a growing place in the modern economy that reaches far beyond the traditional areas of art and culture. Its ability to give added value to brands and products is a major factor in what some writers have called the 'immaterial economy'[1].

In addition, the creation over the past five years of new links between design, management and industry now affect a large number of economic sectors outside the fashion industry in France; these include the cosmetic industry, interior decoration, town planning, multimedia and the automobile industry. In the fashion sector this new economics of design is giving rise to two major phenomena: a rationalisation of the design process that affects both the structures and the people who work in the industry, and the emergence of new specialisations arising out of the need to manage, direct and support design.

This article tackles these phenomena in two stages. The first stage considers the joint development of skills by designers and managers arising both out of the need for greater rationality and the importance now accorded to the added value generated by the fashion houses[2]. The new skills required of both are symptomatic of an urgent need to balance out opposing aptitudes, such as the rational and the emotional or intuition and analytical skills. This work is the result of personal observation based on daily contact with Human Resources Directors and CEOs, and an analysis of the needs in terms of recruitment and contents of the functions and associated skills of recruits. My particular position in IFM allows me to get specific information on careers and job descriptions[3]. In addition, an analysis of emerging skills and jobs was made, referencing job offers received at IFM from March 2002 to February 2004. IFM collected 962 offers during this period.

[1]Authors such as André Gorz (Gorz, 2003) describe a change in capitalism from the material to the immaterial.

[2]In this article 'managers' are understood to mean people with a background in sales or marketing as opposed to 'designers' trained in schools of art or design.

[3]IFM's Career Department receives 500 job offers specialised in the fashion industry per year on average, most of them from French companies.

36

The second part of this article will describe several European training initiatives that aim to back up initial training in these emerging specialisations.

Different worlds that complement one another

The major role of design in today's fashion sector – and the need for companies to rationalise the design process – means that design has to be organised and managed. This consists of adapting design to the market by setting up working structures and in-house operating rules such as scheduling, clearly defined objectives, aids to monitoring fashion collections and sales analysis. While designers are responsible for coming up with concepts and a vision of the world, they need to rely on an individual or a team whose job it is to lay down rules and work structures, as well as to present the designer's concepts to the market and evaluate the risks and the resources needed to develop the concept in terms of marketing and sales. The role of managers should be to provide in-house support and add value to design without taking any direct part in the creative process. The personal approach of managers can be seen as complementary to that of the designers. They need to know about design and understand it in order to better serve and support it; designers for their part need to take on board the constraints imposed by marketing and sales.

The analysis given by Luc Boltanski and Laurent Thévenot (1991) can be taken as a starting-point for an examination of the need for contact and interchange between the different worlds that rub shoulders inside every fashion company[4]. The authors assume that several different worlds coexist: the world of inspiration, the world of family life, the world of political life, the world of commerce and the world of industry. Each of these worlds is defined by characteristics, values (magnitudes) and each has its own specific ways of operating. The authors' approach is one of deconstructing the various elements that make up any organisation in order to make progress in understanding this type of organisation by analysing it as a composite system.

[4]Our approach in this article is sociological and anthropological. Other approaches, particularly those using psychology and neurology, are worth investigating. We might mention the major research programme funded by Antonio Damasio at the University of Iowa, which, among other things, stresses the random separation that has been made down the centuries between body and mind, feelings and reason (1995, 2003).

A fashion company can be defined as a place of necessary compromise between the worlds of inspiration, industry and trade.

The world of inspiration is described as being relatively unstable and subject to changes dictated by the whim of inspiration. This world rejects everything that relates to measuring, rules, money and hierarchies. Inspiration is spontaneous, sudden and chaotic in character. Reality is not directly accessible to the senses and requires special metaphorical language. This world values the state of inspiration, 'illumination, the unsolicited favour' as the authors express it. This inner state is manifested by emotions and passions that inhabit individuals and transform them.

The world of industry is one dominated by technical goals and scientific method. It is dependent upon the efficiency of individuals, their productivity and their ability to respond to precise needs. The 'people of value' in this world are operatives and specialists who are selected for their predictability, reliability and realism. This world rejects everything that is difficult to control such as risks, random events and accidents – just the sort of factors valued in the world of inspiration. One of the risks of the industrial world is that it can become rigid under stress; this is the opposite of what the market demands.

The world of trade is motivated by the desires of individuals who possess the same objects defined by a price. The 'people of value' in this world are those who possess what others desire. The world of trade is composed of individuals seeking to satisfy their desires – customers, competitors, buyers and sellers in turn – and the relations between people are business relations. Transactions presuppose an emotional distance between individuals and situations and control over their emotions which, as we have already seen, constitute value in the world of inspiration, in order to keep the mind clear for recognising business opportunities.

Designers are both dependent on the desires of consumers and on industrial constraints; at the same time these constraints threaten to fetter design in the chains of routine and habit.

The three worlds described here make compromises that enable fashion companies to hold steady without being blown apart. But the balances are sometimes uneasy and sometimes tilt in favour of one world rather than another. The compromise struck between the world of inspiration and the world of trade results in a 'creative market' in which the spontaneous, unexpected appearance of new assets can prove an opportunity for trade-inclined people[5]. The compromise reached between the industrial and creative worlds is predicated on the ability to reconcile passion with efficiency. Passion mobilises potential and the creative energy needed to give improved productivity. The compromise between the industrial world and the trade world is manifested as the product, efficient production characterised by high productivity and the need to satisfy market demand.

But the timeframes of these three worlds are very different. Companies therefore have to impose frameworks and set deadlines on their designers. The managers responsible for this type of supervision need to be capable of understanding design and the creative personality without distorting them, stifling them with constraints or making them crudely subject to market forces that can harm the inherent uniqueness of inspiration. An ongoing, constructive dialogue between the parties is a response to this vital need for compromise between the conflicting values described here. We should note how the very word 'compromise' has changed over the centuries. This is borne out by the special status of artists in the Renaissance who were partially subject to the orders of the patrons who commissioned them[6]. It was this relationship that the change in the status of artists, coupled with a growing, urgent desire for independence, sanctioned throughout the 19th Century in inverse proportion to the rise to power of the industrial sector (Bourdieu, 1992).

Development of specialisations

For several years the brand has been the key strategic factor for companies that target consumers directly[7]. In this context it has now become crucial to define, develop and control the image of companies and their visual identity at every level[8]. A certain rigidity in the design process in the majority of fashion companies has tried to meet this demand for brand identity coherence. By 'the creative process' we mean the entire process from the conception of designs (finding themes and trends and producing sketches of them) through to the creation of collections and their visual presentation in fashion shows, shop windows, catalogues and advertising. Seen more broadly, the creative

[5]We are in the process of becoming consumers of our own lives' (Rifkin, 2000). Fashion holds a key place in this new economy; the classic non-trade factors, whether symbolic, spiritual, affective or emotive, are converted into capital, i.e. human sources of added value.

[6]On this subject see changes in the relationship between artists and their patrons (Heinich, 2000).

[7]Naomi Klein (2000) criticises the negative effects of the rise of the trademark in our economy.

[8]For example, the Gucci Group's website refers to 'the need for absolute coherence of image in each of its brands as well as continuous protection of their integrity'.

process is concerned with the visual world of a brand and what appeals to the consumer's senses and imagination: put another way, the subjective value and the factors that feed this value. This world is not the mere product of the intuition of one or more designers but is essentially the result of strictly applying a set of rules laid down by a creative director or designer intended to ensure the coherence of the collections and visual communication right through to the overall identity of the brand.

Fashion companies are distinguished by their ability to generate added value on the basis of their designs. This being so, competitiveness is centred around the quality of this creative added value and on the ability of companies to communicate their brands.

For this reason, over the last five years the 'communications' function, which originally consisted in public relations operations and the development of contacts with the trade press, has seen its sphere of action enlarged. Today, communication has become a skill used by all the members of the company concerned with the overall brand image. The product constitutes an element of communication on the same footing as advertising, catalogues, fashion shows, boutiques, packaging and the sales staff.

Multi-skilled designers

Today's creative ideas are produced in terms of coherent concepts that define both the position of the brand (product and price), the distribution strategy and the communications policy. Designers working in companies are particularly affected by this change. It is usually the creative director (or designer in a fashion house) who initiates the company's distinguishing concept. This person is also responsible for overseeing compliance with this concept within the company. The creative director often gives the lead concerning design in all its forms without actually designing the collections. He or she has considerable control over all aspects of the brand and is at the very heart of the design process[9]. These new creative directors are often praised for their thoroughness, their marketing skills and their hard-headedness. The management culture now seems to have penetrated the world of design, just as artistic culture has penetrated modern managerial language. The traditional artistic values of desire, intuition and risk are no longer the sole prerogative of designers; they are now

[9] At Yves Saint Laurent, for example, all internal and external documents, whether written or visual, are controlled by a special department that is responsible for overseeing strict compliance with the brand image in direct contact with the artistic director.

also claimed by 'manager-artists' as Luc Boltanski and Eve Chiapello tell us (1999).

From the stylists' point of view, they certainly have to be capable of showing initiative, making artistic choices that will fit into the brand image, but also and most importantly they must be able rigorously to apply the rules laid down by the 'creator'. Stylists working in a design studio are, as it were, the designer's eyes and hands. They have to absorb the brand ethos totally, to the point where they become capable of anticipating the sorts of choices that should be made for particular models – sometimes this is to the detriment of their personal creative vision. But they also have to know how to comply with imperatives of cost, scheduling and organisation laid down by the collection managers. An examination of two stylists' job descriptions, received from French ready-to-wear companies, confirms this view:

Style coordinator (female) (women's ready-to-wear retail company) – January 2004
Highlighting trends with a view to building suitable collections Formalising these trends as strategic guidelines Producing range drawings in terms of shades, materials, shapes and history Drawing up trend books for different markets and targets Validating themes, ranges and scheduling for each stylist/market Advising collection managers and market managers on choice of products and updating Ensuring there are no duplicates in the various markets Ensuring regular reporting to the market manager and collection manager
Training: design school **Profile:** strong marketing sense more important than creativity; organised, rigorous, methodical

Stylist (women's ready-to-wear – creative brand) – December 2003
You will report to the style manager. You will participate in designing and working up the collection plan with the rest of the team. You will comply with the product and marketing plan. You will construct style boards, suggest themes, develop new forms, materials, sketches and colour ranges that adapt trends to the needs of the brand.
Training: fashion design – model making Profile: must get on well with people, good artistic sense, you must be able to combine good taste with a sound business sense.

These job descriptions can be seen as true examples of what is required in job offers we receive at IFM. They are representative enough to illustrate the kind of skills that are always mentioned by French companies. We have kept the exact words which were used in the job offers in order to compare them and analyse the needs of French companies.

It is clear that the terms really belong to the vocabulary used to describe the application of rules of procedure. Sales and marketing skills appear to be required for these types of profile even though the training backgrounds required in the advertisements are creative ones. More generally, coordination skills, an understanding of the market, the ability to analyse critically and leadership skills are vital requirements.

We can see that the new skills required to tackle creative specialisations are disparate, even contradictory: an ability to create new and original concepts, an ability to open one's creative scope to include a variety of media (collections, by-products, boutiques, visuals, etc.), the power to influence but also the ability to adapt to a different creative environment than one's own, an ability to stick to rules, an ability to analyse situations and to be meticulous, a feeling for the market and the realities of industry.

What is more, today's stylists who are working in the context of imposed design often become the designers of the future, initiating concepts and taking responsibility for the visual identity of their brand or that of the company they work for. The consequences in terms of the training and skills that need developing must obviously be taken on board.

Nowadays the range of specialisations on offer to designers when they leave college is wider that it used to be. In fact, even though the status of salaried or freelance designers working in a studio remains the commonest choice, new specialisations are emerging that can be practised by either designers or managers. For example, a post as a visual merchandiser can be filled equally well by a designer or a marketing specialist. This is because employers have often not accurately defined the specific skills required by these specialisations and tend to base their choice more on character traits than on training.

Managers open to design

Just as designers have to be aware of the importance of the concept and overall communication of a brand, managers have to know how to support and understand design without inhibiting it. This is the price design companies have to pay for their added value.

The ability of a manager to take design on board, include the world of creation and understand the way it operates is a key factor for success. It is often the manager who has to explain design to the various other players: suppliers, sellers and consumers. The specifications or 'brief' drawn up by the manager for the designer or studio with which he or she is working constitute a key stage in the design process. Both the form and content of this brief have a determining influence on building a common language. Throughout the rest of the process the quality of the dialogue between managers and designers is vital for the balance and coherence of the collections. But this ongoing dialogue is not entirely risk-free.

At the present time we are seeing people from a number of different fields encroaching on the field of design; this creates hybrid areas where role-definitions can be hazy. Intelligent division of responsibility and constructive dialogue between the different specialisations is vital if companies are to succeed.

Training projects in the pipeline

In order to keep up with the development of skills associated with the emergence of these new functions, a number of training initiatives are currently under way. These consist, on the one hand, of new ways of initiating students in marketing, project management and personal development and are gradually being included in a number of design training programmes. On the other hand, we should mention certain original courses that have been launched in recent years that aim to give students a broad, personal grasp of the design sector.

The *Università Dell Imagine* or 'University of the five senses' in Milan is a two-year programme that prepares students in the various specialisations related to image and communications. This programme, which was founded in 1998 by the photographer and entrepreneur Fabrizio Ferri, is original in that it is built around the concept of the five senses: sight, smell, hearing, touch and taste. Teaching is based on exercises, theoretical sessions and the running of individual projects aimed at developing the relations between ethics and aesthetics and strengthening students' primary, authentic sensitivity. The school is based on the union of a particular conception of creativity and the conviction that creativity must be made understood. The school chooses and trains creative personalities to develop projects that use the five senses to create different types of overall image. The school aims not so much at using particular techniques to turn students into specialists as developing their individual creative abilities to serve company projects. This training prepares students for a number of different specialisations: Photographer, Creative Marketing in Prestige Goods, Food and Wine Critic, Creative Director, Art Director, Perfumer ('Nose'), Packaging Designer, Fragrance Development Manager, Photo Editor, etc. The text presenting the school states: 'Image is the global language of the new millennium'. A 'Laboratory of the Senses' has been set up to support students' projects and complement the research work performed by the teaching staff. This laboratory is divided up into distinct sections for each of the five senses. The students devise projects in partnership with businesses and cover every kind of applied design: creation and launch of new perfumes, olfactory projects related to art, visual proposals for magazines (graphic concept and realisation), concepts for promotional and artistic events for specific trade fairs, salons or exhibitions, and so on. Over and above the teaching of specific technical skills, the course aims at developing a general attitude, and a certain open-mindedness, which is placed at a premium. The main aim of the programme is to enable students to use a variety of techniques and leave the beaten track in an approach that is both creative and entrepreneurial. One of the dangers of this approach, however, is that students may have too broad a vision; they may become too multi-skilled and the course may produce graduates who are certainly open and innovative but lacking in distinctive, directly operational skills. This type of approach is better used with professionals who already have a certain amount of technical experience under their belts but who are now looking for a broader view, than with beginners who are only starting out in the field of design.

In an attempt to encourage dialogue between the 'emotional' and the 'rational' among young professionals, the French Fashion Institute bases some of its teaching on 'cohabitation' between the two

44

postgraduate programmes, i.e. the specialist management course and the international design course[10]. This type of coexistence gives students a chance to develop the abilities of managers and designers to speak one another's language. To achieve this, a series of workshops is organised based around collective projects to develop a collection. The students work in teams of four or five managers with a single designer. The objective of the workshops is to enable students to develop a collection based on a design concept by jointly drawing up the strategic positioning and all the components of the marketing mix (products, price, distribution and communication), as well as the short- and medium-term business plans.

After an initial phase to allow managers to get a grasp of how the creative world functions, together with a joint attempt by the members of the team to come up with common definitions of the key words characterising this world, the group jointly prepares an overall presentation of the collection and the strategic decisions for the development of the brand. At the same time as the design work itself, the students are encouraged throughout the exercise to be aware of how they operate in terms of human relations and teamwork. In particular they have to try and analyse the following factors:

- the division of work between managers and designers; management of time;
- how managers approach understanding the creative world;
- the balance between the demands and priorities of costs, pattern of production, stylistic choices, communication;
- the contribution of each team member, both managers and designers;
- possible improvements in how the team functions;
- skills developed by the workshop itself.

On completion of the workshop the students are encouraged to express themselves on these questions in debriefings conducted in small groups.

A few 'keys to success' may emerge from the first analyses undertaken by the groups.[11] Tasks should be divided up on the basis of the skills of each member of the group and not, as is too often the case, based on personal preferences. Moreover, clearly defined territories, which

[10]It should be pointed out that the IFM's advanced programmes are solely for postgraduate students.

implies genuine respect for the other members' skills, is one of the keys to the success of the exercise. Furthermore, laying down clear rules of work from the very start of the project also enables students to make the best of the time spent in workshops. But it is essentially on questions of the ability to understand the creative world and strategic compromises that the students are able to measure the real impact of constructive dialogue between managers and designers.

This stage has proved crucial in creating a positive working environment. An atmosphere of trust is laid down at this stage. Sometimes it has even been found that this stage has helped to resolve situations that have reached a dead end due to unexpressed feelings or lack of communication.

Often, if a designer feels at ease and abides by the jointly selected keywords defining his or her world, teamwork becomes possible. The validation of this phase often requires the intervention of a legitimising third party, in the present case, the tutor. Managers have also found it helpful to discover the designer's world by means of images, sounds and a range of miscellaneous references without having to base their perceptions solely on explanations or input provided by the designer; such explanations sometimes tend to hide behind clichés in order to preserve a certain air of mystery or to protect the designer's inner self.

The question of a split or a merging of managers and designers is another key factor. Often initial merging enables dialogue and common thinking between individuals who have been brought together at random. But in some cases excessive merging can harm objectivity. Managers can become partisans of a designer's work and lose the ability to make critical analyses of the strategy that should be developed.

Sometimes managers' and designers' interests are so far apart that no common ground can be found. The designer can feel completely detached from the work and no longer takes any real part in the exercise. Maintaining an ongoing dialogue between the members of the team is the surest way of evaluating the motivation of each member and clearing any obstacles that may arise.

'We let him not get involved,' and 'We answered questions for him,' are both ways of sidelining designers, often in an attempt to protect them.

[1]IFM have only been using workshops since 2002.

46

This type of group work is sometimes an opportunity for designers to express themselves and explain their world more intelligibly. This exercise often helps designers to use more conceptual language, particularly where the designer in question is essentially sensitive and more inclined to work on the basis of sensations or emotions than clearly defined concepts. Finally, in addition to developing collections tailored to suit a particular market, these workshops encourage a coming together of the rational and the emotional; this may occur for particular individuals, but initially take place with the group. The collective experience of this encounter is an interesting phase in personal development[12] as well as in the construction of a shared view. It prepares students for the task of managing creative projects they will have to undertake in businesses in the sector. The experience of surviving difficulties and the successes of this type of collaboration help both types of individual to develop a common language and mutual understanding.

At a regional level, the experience initiated by the Artem project is similar in spirit, based as it is on an attempt to bring about a moving closer between training and specialisations that usually have little contact with one another. The Artem label is, in fact, the result of an alliance between disciplines that are usually in opposition to one another: the sciences, technology and the arts. This alliance brings together the National School of Advanced Art Studies (Ecole Nationale Supérieure d'Art), the National School of Advanced Mining Studies (Ecole Supérieure des Mines) and the ICN business school, all three located in Nancy, France. The programme is characterised by its innovative teaching and research project. The name of the project says it all: the word '*Artem*' is the accusative form of the Latin noun '*ars*', meaning talent, craft, profession and technique, but also law, rule or method; all this boils down to applied know-how. For the founders of Artem, training individuals in a way that is fragmented, broken down into a multitude of tiny tasks (as in a time and motion approach), over-specialised and lacking any broader knowledge is meaningless. They view as sterile, even dangerous, the dichotomy exercised by educational systems that separate the teaching of the so-called humanities and creativity from instruction in the sciences and technology.

[12]On this subject, see Boltanski and Chiapello *Le nouvel esprit du capitalisme* (The New Spirit of Capitalism) (1999), which looks at cities in terms of projects where individualism becomes an intrinsic value of the new network economy.

In practical terms, every student at the schools belonging to the alliance will be able to choose courses run outside his or her core school. The range of training offered to each student is therefore enriched. This training initiative also offers students a dual qualification, thereby also giving them twice the skills[13].

The Artem training is also based on a management simulation game that, by managing a project, enables students to tackle fields remote from their core skills. The game consists of working as a team to design a product and launch it on the market; the game ensures a good balance between the artistic, economic and technical fields.

The other innovatory teaching approach at Artem is the creation of workshops that students can choose individually. Nearly 20 workshops are available at the three schools participating in the alliance. Approximately 30% of students choose a workshop outside their core field of training. This initiative is an interesting approach that encourages openness and interdisciplinary dialogue, particularly between fields that tend to be in conflict. This touches the very heart of the exchange between emotional intelligence and more rational types of thinking. Engineering, arts and business students all learn from one another. Over and above theoretical learning, it is the meeting of personalities and traditionally disparate modes of thought that makes for an interesting cognitive experience.

We can see that the opportunities in terms of the specialisations open to students at schools of fashion and design are increasing rapidly. Over and above the acquisition of theoretical or technical skills, it is essentially the learning of attitudes appropriate to different people and different situations that constitutes a guarantee of success for professionals in this sector. The tendency towards decompartmentalisation, non-specialisation, openness and the development of strong personalities is vital for both the managers and the designers of tomorrow. But there are many limits on the abolition of all compartmentalisation. While it is true that designers should be capable of understanding the constraints and risks of the marketplace, they must be careful not to see themselves as fashion-industry 'super-specialists'. There is a strong temptation for some people to see themselves, or to see others, as the real directors of

[13]The dual qualification is only awarded by the Engineering and Business schools.

48

businesses, basing their success on the value of their design. We have seen that the omnipotence of certain creative directors may prove dangerous both for design itself and for the economy and survival of certain companies[14]. On the other hand, in an attempt to take over the design role, some managers may be tempted to do away with designers and overestimate their intuitive and emotional intelligence. While 'flair' remains something that good managers need to develop, it cannot replace the special vision and inherent skills required for creation.

The training project towards which the schools are tending is, in the final analysis, based on the development of a culture of exchange that does not break down specialities but, on the contrary, encourages the building of bridges between skills that are complementary and distinctive.

References

Boltanski, L. & Chiapello, E. (1999), *Le nouvel esprit du capitalisme* (Paris: Gallimard)

Boltanski, L. & Thevenot, L. (1991), *De la justification les économies de la grandeur* (Paris: Gallimard)

Bourdieu, P. (1992), *Les règles de l'art* (Paris: Seuil)

Damasio, A.R. (1995), Descartes' Error: Emotion, Reason, and the Human Brain (New York: Avon)

Damasio, A.R. (2003), *Looking for Spinoza: Joy, Sorrow, and The Feeling Brain* (Orlando: Hartcourt)

Gorz, A. (2003), *L'immatériel* (Paris: Galilée)

Heinich, N. (1993), *Du peintre à l'artiste, Artisans et académiciens à l'âge classique* (Paris: Minuit)

Klein, N. (2000), *No Logo* (Paris: Actes Sud)

Rifkin, J. (2000), *The Age of Access: The New Culture of Hypercapitalism, Where All of Life Is Paid-For Experience* (New York: J.P. Tarcher)

[14]We could cite the case of Tom Ford who single-handedly controlled all decisions about the identity of the Yves Saint Laurent and Gucci brands and whose departure from the two firms has raised real fears as to who can keep the design flag flying.

Biographical note

A graduate of IECS and IFM, **Karine Piotraut** holds a postgraduate degree in Corporate Policies on Social Development and Employment from Science-Po Paris and has worked for several years in the Accessories Department for Christian Lacroix. She then joined the Framatome Group as Head of the Human Resources Department for its La Défense headquarters. She is presently with IFM in charge of Industrial Relations, Job Placement and Career Development for students and alumni.

Institut Français de la Mode was established in 1986 as a centre for education and expertise for professionals in the textile and fashion industry. It is involved in two major fields of activity: Education and Economic Trends & Market Research.

The Education Division is structured around the two postgraduate programmes (in management and fashion design) as well as the Professional Training programmes and the Publishing Department. The Textile and Fashion Management postgraduate programme (French government classification level 1), focuses on decompartmentalisation between functions and disciplines, close contact with the industry and internationalisation. Nearly 800 alumni who have graduated from this programme hold high-level jobs across the whole sector. The International Fashion Design postgraduate programme, the first postgraduate programme of its kind in France, started in January 2000 and is training tomorrow's fashion designers and art directors. Assimilating the fabrication process and the demands of management without losing the power of the creative idea is the essential ambition of this programme.

Karine Piotraut teaches methodology related to job research and career development to the students of both programmes.

Developing communication skills through fashion design

Alison Shreeve and Carmel Kelly
London College of Fashion, London, UK

Introduction

Education in the UK, for design-based subjects such as fashion, has evolved from a very practical, grounded approach in developing skills and knowledge about the subject. This might be termed an experiential approach (Kolb) or one in which 'making and doing' is central to the learning activity. Even where developing design skills is the intention, a course is normally centred around the practical processes or skills components of the manufacturing and construction of garments. This is usually supplemented with a range of supporting areas from marketing, business, management, cultural awareness, contextual and historical studies and actual work experience, which complement the more process- and materials-based activities of the curriculum.

It is the essentially practical nature of learning in the college that actually provides a very secure basis for developing skills that are not quite so obvious. Within the UK there has been a drive for the assessment of 'common skills', or 'key skills'; those more generic, non subject-specific attributes which are particularly cited by employers as essential requirements of their new graduate workforce. The National Committee of Inquiry into Higher Education, which reported in 1997 (the Dearing Report), listed the skills of communication, numeracy, Information Technology (IT) and Learning to Learn as key skills for the development of a learning society. Since then, these skills have been an assessed part of most higher education courses within the UK sector. An investigation into the way key skills were being developed in the materials technology and art and design subject areas found that there were many different approaches to this assessment and that students were not always aware of when these skills were being assessed (the Keynote Project).

Within the Keynote Project, communication is defined as taking a number of forms within the curriculum:

- written communication (essays, reports);
- verbal communication (one-to-one and presentations to groups);
- listening skills;
- visual communication (drawing and layout); and
- presentation skills.

Within fashion design, the skills of communication are not necessarily the same as those required for communicating in any other discipline, as the language of fashion is perhaps particular in many ways to the discipline itself.

Central to the core of the fashion design process is the fact that communication is primarily visual. This visual medium may be based on paper, on a computer screen or through garments themselves. Each area or aspect of communication has its own common dialect or conventions, which need to be learned. Whilst these visual mediums and functions may have verbal labels, such as 'flats' or 'flat drawings' the understanding of these meanings is developed through social interaction in a subject- or work-based context, that includes these visual materials. The precise formats of such materials are social constructions that evolve over time as the participants engage in learning within social groups (Lave & Wenger, 1991; Wenger, 2000) and also as fashion and technology change and develop. The language is not static, but is subject to local variation and common practices. Even within a social group or practice, individuals may have very different perceptions of situations and different intentions underlying their activities (Marton & Booth, 1997).

Studies into the way fashion students approach their learning in project work have identified that there are qualitatively different ways in which this might be experienced (Drew et al., 2003). Only through encouragement to explore more inclusive and comprehensive ways of experiencing will students be enabled to develop more in-depth or complex approaches to their design studies. Although this research only looked at approaches to learning and the research component of the fashion project (Shreeve et al., 2004), it is likely that similar differences will occur in the way the communicative aspects of the design process are approached and understood.

The whole process of generation of ideas through design to manufacture is primarily centred on the visual manipulation and conveyance of information. This information could be said to be constructed by one person, with the intention of conveying a series of messages to another person who should act upon that information in a specific way, preferably that intended by the originator of the information. At its simplest level communication could be illustrated thus:

message   =   transmission   =   reception

However, what is to be conveyed is an intended meaning, which may or may not be received, experienced or interpreted in the way the sender intended it to be.

Both the sender and receiver of information need to speak the same language at the very least in order for the message to be understood. The visual conventions of fashion design and manufacture are also a language, which both receiver and sender need to be able to read and understand. This pertains to the end product, which is never simply neutral, but has social meaning and significance, and also within the design and making of the product where practitioners and key people within the production process also need to be aware of the wider contexts and sets of meanings related to the product. The visual, as opposed to the written word, is subject to more variation in meaning, or as Penn (2000) argues, 'the image is always polysemic or ambiguous' (p. 229), which is why the conventions of a visual language must be learned within a particular context.

A project was developed with a group of second-year students on a higher education fashion design and technology course, with the intention of developing their awareness of the importance of communication and to improve their skills of communication within the subject area. Central to this intention was the belief that none of these students would ever be working in isolation and few would be undertaking the whole process of fashion design, through original idea to finished product. Whatever role they undertook in the industry, teamwork and communication with others would be necessary.

The project design

The project was based on each individual student developing a series of ideas based around a fashion prediction theme. They were required to develop their ideas for a specific market, with a target age, consumer profile and retailer in mind. The 'normal' expectations of the design project were undertaken individually at this point. After research into the parameters of the project, the market, the garment type, fabrics, the conceptual ideas about the social and cultural meaning and referents surrounding the design ideas, the student constructed a series of visuals that included a mood board, which sets the overall feeling of the design. In the mood board the colour palette, atmosphere and emotion of the design is conveyed through a collection of images selected to summarise what the end product is to convey to the consumer. At this point it is fundamentally an abstract idea, a concept, which has then to be transformed into a wearable item. This is achieved through the process of roughs – developed themes exploring garment type, shape, volume, detail and structure – until a significant design is reached that fulfils the requirements of the design set by the parameters of the project brief and the individual interpretation of this by the student. The identification of suitable fabrics is considered to be at the heart of successful designing and the awareness of the properties and handle of fabrics is well developed in professional designers and pattern cutters. Understanding the properties of the fabric, or selecting an appropriate fabric to perform a particular desired function, is an essential part of the information, which should be part of the communication process in the design and production of garments.

At this point in the fashion design project the normal procedure would be for the student to begin to construct a flat pattern, or to work through draping on the stand, to develop their flat design intention into a viable product. We consider this to be an important way to continue to develop design ideas; the process being open to experimentation, questioning and inspiration until a 'finished' design is reached. Developing and testing ideas in the round, in three dimensions, allows judgements to be made and possibilities to be seen which in a smaller and flatter dimension are not always evident. However, in this case we asked the student to suspend his or her involvement with the design work at the stage of constructing a 'flat' working drawing of the design. The flat is intended as a technical blueprint for the next stage of the manufacturing process, the pattern cutting. In order to supplement the information we also asked the student to produce a 'finished' drawing of the intended design. This is more akin to the mood board, where the garment is drawn with a sense of feeling, movement, three dimensions and atmosphere.

At this stage the students started working in groups of three. We asked the designer and producer of the 'flat' drawing to pass that and their finished design drawing to someone else; they in turn received drawings from a colleague and were then asked to construct a finished pattern for that design. Having completed the garment pattern pieces they then had to pass the pattern to a third person who was asked to make up a toile using the flat pattern and the working drawing. Thus each student took on the role of designer, pattern cutter and sample machinist within the same project. At each stage of the project the students were asked to evaluate the effectiveness of the communication they received, to itemise their difficulties in reading the information and list incomplete or missing areas of information conveyed to them. At the end of the project the toiles were put on the stand and evaluated against the original design drawing by all three participants, who discussed the process and outcomes of the project and evaluated and articulated the aspects of the communication stages and their effect on the outcomes.

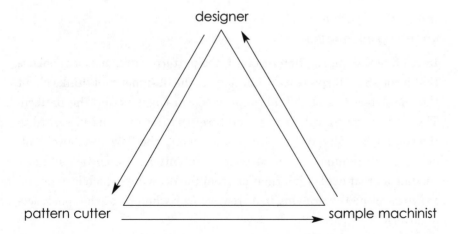

Figure 1 The three roles undertaken by each student throughout the project

Communication development within the stages of the project

Throughout the project students were actively engaged in both constructing and acting upon visual and technical information and they were also asked to reflect upon the process of communication as they encountered it.

The designer
Communicating information

For the designer to successfully communicate his or her intention to a pattern cutter through the working drawing and the finished drawing, the two forms of communication need to be quite different in their modes and language. The technical information needs to be precise, in proportion, provide style lines where seams will be positioned, details of finishing and fastenings and some idea of the drape or hang of the fabric, though this needs to be tempered by the precision of the cut. It is expected that a swatch of fabric will be provided at this point as being a key component of the information. It is noted, however, that students often do not have a particular fabric in mind when they design and this was the case for some participants in this project. Supplementary information can be provided with annotations in words and measurements, which add to the information of the line drawing. The finished drawing, on the other hand, will be more fluid in suggesting the volume, movement and mood of the finished garment – the designer's ultimate intention for the viewer and wearer.

The pattern cutter
Receiving information

In reading the information received, the pattern cutter needs to ensure that he or she interprets the intentions of the designer and thinks about the characteristics of the fabric provided in constructing the pattern. The pattern cutter will need to interpret the flat drawing in regard to the volume and shape of the finished garment, the flow and movement, or restraint, required by the designer's intention. The cutter is in fact reading a great deal of information from the drawing, which is essential to interpreting the drawing in a creative way when he or she constructs a pattern.

Communicating information

The first pattern is an important stage in the process and has to be carefully and methodically produced. The measurements need to be accurate and precise and pieces need to match in the right places. The grain lines will inform the cutter how the pattern pieces are to be laid on the fabric and the pattern piece balance marks will inform the machinist of the sequence of stitching piece to piece. Any lack of information at this point leads to poor interpretation and impossible situations when the machinist comes to construct the pieces into their final form.

The sample machinist
Receiving information

The sample machinist receives the pattern from the pattern cutter and proceeds to make up the first toile of the garment. If the full information about the linings, interlinings, fabric, fastenings and finishings is provided the machinist may have a fairly straightforward job. There may be decisions to be made about the right fabric to use for the toile or prototype, the thread type, machines to use, stitch length and tension adjustments.

Communicating information

The fabric for the toile, the finishes chosen by the machinist and the skill of manufacture all speak about the interpretation of the pattern and working drawing provided by the pattern cutter. The final toile should match the kind of intentions that have been provided by the designer. If all communication has been sensitive, clearly articulated and accurately interpreted throughout the stages the final three-dimensional product should be a good translation of the idea into reality.

The designer, pattern cutter and machinist are not working within a vacuum, but need to be attuned to the context of their communication process. They need to be aware of the current visual discussions and debates about fashion. The market level, which they are working within, will also dictate how the information is to be acted upon or interpreted. When radical ideas surface or new technology becomes available the whole range of appropriate decisions within a fashion context expands or shifts to accommodate the changes. The language of communication within the world of fashion is used by a wide and global community. Far from being an isolated genius, the designer is part of a society in which they need to be able to communicate through, with and about the visual, verbal and material milieu of their world.

Evaluation

At every stage of the project the students were asked to evaluate how they found the interpretation or reading of the information they received. They were asked to think about why they found some things difficult to do and what would have made the process easier. They wrote down their evaluation and at the end of the project the group came together to see the results of the process, with all three people who had contributed, from the idea to the realisation of the design. At this point they were asked to compare the toile with the finished drawing and evaluate how well the garment resembled the intention of the designer and what might have led to the differences they could see between the intention and the reality of the garment. They were also asked to talk about the importance of conveying particular aspects of the information, and where they found it hard to understand what was intended and why they found this hard. They were thus required to relate the visual and material aspects of the communication process to verbal articulation, making explicit the non-verbal communication processes.

Learning through the experience
Assessment

One of the most important factors that influence learning is the timing and form of assessment (Gibbs, 2003). Understanding the assessment process is not necessarily a transparent and unproblematic process for students. They will tend to approach the way they learn depending on the way they perceive the assessment task (Laurillard, 1984). With assessment in this project being centred on the students and their experiences we designed the learning task to incorporate the need to evaluate communication. We followed this through with interactive assessment in which the students also participated, thus the intention of the learning, the design of the learning activity and the assessment were aligned (Biggs, 1996). As a group, the students were asked to evaluate the process of communication as they had experienced it within the project. They could then perceive through other's eyes how their communication had been interpreted and evaluate differences between their assumptions and the received information.

In addition to talking about the stages of interpreting the design, the students were asked to fill out an evaluation sheet using criteria for assessment that would be used by the academics to determine the final assessment grade for the work submitted. This interaction with evaluative criteria also leads to an increase in understanding of the kinds of evaluations made about fashion design work, including the function of communicating to others, which is inherent in this process. The students were asked at each stage of the project to evaluate the efficacy of the information they received. Could they act upon it? Were intentions clear? Where did they have problems in understanding or interpreting information that they were supposed to act upon? Asking students to reflect on their situation both guides them and encourages them to become independent and more confident in being critical in evaluating and questioning for themselves.

The students participate in the assessment process. They are provided with a list of statements, which form the basis for evaluating the work. They use these evaluations to discuss the performance of each participant throughout the stages of the project. Through linking words and phrases to the practical aspects of the project the students increase their awareness of the factors that are critical to effective communication in design. They develop improved understanding of the functions of the different forms of drawn and written communication and also practice their skills of verbalising these critical factors.

The questions were framed to make explicit the kinds of knowledge held by specialists and the judgements made by tutors or specialists, as they would evaluate the products and processes. This provides language and vocabulary in association with the concrete experience, which allows what might remain tacit to become accessible and articulated. Making the tacit explicit leads to increased confidence (Freeman, 1991). In examples of traditional assessment, with unseen examination papers, students actively seek cues as to what might be on the paper (Miller and Parlett, 1974) – those who are skilled in detecting what might be used to test them are more successful. Unlike in traditional assessment practices, here the students are made a party to the language of assessment and evaluation processes and are encouraged to articulate these phrases and engage in the process for themselves. The tutor acts as a guide here to prompt and link the words on the paper to the actual reality of the toile. Questions arise in discussion about the relationship between the drawings and the sketch. The designer is present too and keen to ask why the result doesn't match what he or she had in mind when the project began. For some students the process has been very successful and they are pleased with the result. Here the team can track back and support the reasons why they all succeeded in realising in three dimensions what was an idea on paper, a communication of intent, an abstract idea.

Conclusion

Through having to act on others' communications, and having to communicate in different aspects of the design project, students are encouraged to develop meaning in relation to the design process. The drawing is no longer a private function but becomes a communication tool, which mirrors the reality of this function in the world of employment.

The practical nature of fashion education here provides a sound basis for providing opportunities to develop communication skills. This is an illustration of the stages required in Kolb's learning cycle. The abstract development of a design concept is realised, that is, made concrete, through a process of experimentation. The requirement to then reflect on this process, which we ask the students to undertake at each stage of role play, is also enhanced through the assessment process. This provides opportunities for both reflection on their own learning and the learning of communication skills as demonstrated by others, thus providing opportunities for vicarious learning.

Far from being a separately taught set of skills, communication skills become meaningful, realistic and very much a central requirement of the fashion design process through the enhancement of role play and active participation in assessment.

References

Biggs, J. (1996), 'Enhancing teaching through constructive alignment', *Higher Education*, 32, pp. 347-364

Drew, L., Shreeve, A. & Bailey, S. (2003), 'Fashion variations: students' approaches to learning in fashion design', in *Enhancing Curricula: Exploring effective curricula practices in art design and communication in Higher Education*, pp. 179-198 (London: Centre for Learning and Teaching in Art and Design)

Freeman, D. (1991), 'To make the tacit explicit – teacher education, emerging discourse and conceptions of teaching', *Journal of Teaching and Teacher Education*, 7, 5-6, pp. 439-454

Kolb, D.A. (1984), Experiential Learning: Experience as the source of learning and development (Eaglewood Cliffs, New Jersey: Prentice-Hall)

Lave, J. & Wenger, E. (1991), *Situated Learning: Legitimate peripheral participation* (Cambridge: Cambridge University Press)

Marton, F. & Booth, S. (1997), *Learning and Awareness* (Mahwah, New Jersey: Lawrence Erlbaum)

Miller, C.M.L. & Parlett, M.R. (1974), *Up To The Mark: A study of the examination game* (London: Society for Research into Higher Education)

Penn, G. (2000), 'Semiotic analysis of still images', in Bauer, M. & Gaskell, G. (eds.) *Qualitative Researching with Text Image and Sound* (London, New Delhi and Thousand Oaks: Sage)

Prosser, M. & Trigwell, K. (1999), *Understanding Learning and Teaching* (Buckingham: SRHE and Open University Press)

Ramsden, P. (1992), *Learning to Teach in Higher Education* (London: Routledge)

Shreeve, A., Bailey, S. & Drew, L. (2004), 'Students' approaches to the "research" component in the fashion design project: variation in students' experience of the research process', *Journal of Art, Design and Communication in Higher Education*, 2, 3 pp. 113-130

The Keynote Project (2001), http://www.leeds.ac.uk/textiles/keynote

Wenger, E. (2000), *Communities of Practice: Learning, meaning and identity* (Cambridge: Cambridge University Press)

62

Biographical notes

Alison Shreeve. My first degree was in Fashion Textiles, with Embroidery as the chief area of study, and I have taught this subject to a range of students on different courses in post compulsory education in the UK. My interests include the social construction of meaning and the role of textiles in everyday life. This extends also to the teaching and learning of these subjects in more formal educational contexts.

I am currently Director of the Creative Learning in Practice Centre for Excellence in Teaching and Learning (CLIP CETL), at the University of the Arts London. The centre is funded for five years by the Higher Education Funding Council for England and is a teaching and learning enhancement initiative, one of 72 centres throughout England. The CLIP CETL is a joint venture between Chelsea College of Art and Design and London College of Fashion, two of the constituent colleges of UAL. Its activities will explore the nature of practice-based learning and the relationship of the student experience to employment in the creative industries.

Carmel Kelly. My background comprises a combination of industrial experience and teaching. Originally gaining qualifications as a Fashion Designer Pattern Cutter I entered the world of work, progressing my career from assistant to designer for a company selling to high street chains. From this I moved into consultancy work and running my own design and manufacturing business. During this period I began lecturing, later working overseas on UNDP projects and finally taking up a full-time role in education in 1995. My interest in developing key transferable and lifelong learning skills stems from my years in industry when I realised that without good communication skills a person's ability to grow and develop is hampered.

I am a Principal Lecturer and International Consultant at London College of Fashion. Currently based in Sri Lanka, I am engaged in a consultancy project with the University of Moratuwa, Sri Lanka. This is a management and development role, setting up a four-year sandwich degree course tailor-made for Sri Lankan students, with close liaison with industry in the region. This role also includes staff development in learning and teaching pertinent to practical subjects in a university environment.

London College of Fashion is part of University of the Arts London, which comprises five highly acclaimed colleges of art, design and communications.

LCF was established in 1906 to provide specialist education and training for the fashion industry. Its rich history has enabled the college to offer a unique portfolio of courses ranging from foundation to undergraduate to postgraduate and research degree level that reflect the breadth of opportunities available in the vibrant and ever-changing fashion and creative industries. We have a bourgeoning research culture that crosses the boundaries between industry and academia.

The college works collaboratively with major museums and galleries, including the Victoria and Albert Museum, and has a range of international partnerships. The location affords students all the cultural benefits and resources associated with a major city and extensive industry links provide a rich exchange and collaboration for learning. The college is committed to career-focused education for its students, encouraging them to be creative while providing them with the expertise and facilities to turn their visions into reality.

The transformation of the Fashion Merchandising programme: from teacher-centred to student-centred pedagogy

Betty Li Shu Wan
The Hong Kong Polytechnic University, Hong Kong

Abstract

The course of Fashion Merchandising at Hong Kong Plytechnic University has a strong vocational nature. The course content relates directly to the merchandising field of fashion business and it aims to prepare students with knowledge and skills for related jobs. The traditional teaching approach is found to be ineffective in achieving such a purpose. Originating from medical education, problem-based learning (PBL) has been increasingly used in other professional education. Tempted by many successful experiences, we have taken a bold step in transforming the traditional teacher-centred pedagogy to problem-based learning. The use of this new approach has brought about a revolution in the whole curriculum and in the ways that the teacher teaches and student learns.

The new teaching approach guides the reform of the course structure and delivery. Instead of the use of lectures as the major means of transmitting the compartmentalised knowledge areas, the student-centred curriculum is structured basically by problem cases that drive learning. With each problem case addressing certain knowledge areas, students are initiated to learn through various sources, apply and integrate knowledge in different areas. In collaboration with the merchandising practitioners, the problem cases were written up to resemble a contemporary working environment. In the process of running the problem cases, students are put in the positions of real-life merchandising personnel. Students are expected to recognise needs to learn in order to solve problems. This recognition initiates self-directed learning instead of the one-way passive feeding of knowledge through scheduled lectures. In addition to the learning of knowledge, students also acquire transferable skills that are necessary for merchandising jobs. No approach can be considered to be perfect. Although student feedback on the course has been found to be encouraging, adjustments need to be made for continuous improvement.

Introduction

Fashion Merchandising is a course with a high work-related content. With the transformation of Hong Kong into a service centre, a significant proportion of graduates from the Institute of Textiles and Clothing worked in the merchandising field. Fresh graduates would mainly take up junior posts in merchandising, such as assistant merchandisers or merchandising trainees in textile and apparel firms. As such, the course of Fashion Merchandising has a clear direction in preparing students for the career of merchandiser in general. Hong Kong's merchandisers are the central coordinators linking all the parties and activities in supplying merchandise to the buyers. In the actual working environment, merchandisers always face problems arising from the merchandise supply. Success depends very much on a merchandiser's ability to solve these problems. In addition to the problem-solving skill, there is a high demand for merchandisers to be equipped with skills in communication, presentation, teamwork and research.

Problem-based learning (PBL) as a type of student-centred pedagogic approach has received much attention in recent decades and has a wide application in many professional education areas such as medicine, business administration, engineering and nursing (Bridges & Hallinger, 1991; Williams & Williams, 1997; Boud & Feletti, 1991). The effectiveness of this pedagogy is well documented and the reported benefits accrued to the students include the development of a self-motivated learning attitude, the ability to recall, integrate and apply knowledge in problem solving, the skill of handling interpersonal relationships and teamwork (Vernon, 1995; Norman & Schmidt, 1992; Schmidt, Norman & Boshuizen, 1990; Morrison, 2004). Tempted by the success in these fields in generating student quality, which is much required in the field of merchandising, a bold step was made in 2000 to introduce the new pedagogy in the course of Fashion Merchandising.

In fashion education, pedagogy represents a neglected area of discussion and research. Most of the related literature focuses on the education system providing fashion-related programmes (e.g. Ladchumananandasivam & de Medeiros, 1999; Mock, 2000; Rusu, 1996; Richards, 1996), education-industry partnership in training students (e.g. Priest, 1995; Kellomaki & Pesoneu, 1996) and teaching technology (e.g. Hari, Goyal & Behera, 2002; Lam & McCabe, 1997). Although some research has been done to investigate the job-related competencies and knowledge of students required by the fashion business, it contributes basically to the programme or course content (e.g. Greenwood, 1981; Fair, Hamilton & Norum, 1990; Kelly, 1980). Until recently, pedagogic issues have emerged to be a topic of study in textile education. Garde, Kane & Mahajan (2000) of the Textile and Engineering Institute proposed a student-centred learning approach to replace the traditional teaching mode in textile degree programmes. Taylor (1999) made an attempt to introduce case-based and problem-based programmes to help students develop problem-solving skills applicable to the textile industry. Less is known, however, about the course structure and delivery in relation to the pedagogy and its effectiveness in textile-related programmes.

This paper represents one of the first attempts made to describe and assess the use of a student-centred pedagogic approach in the course of Fashion Merchandising. It is composed of four parts:

- the job-related competence required for merchandisers;
- the rationale of student-centred pedagogy;
- the use of the student-centred pedagogy in the course of Fashion Merchandising; and
- the assessment of the effectiveness of student-centred pedagogy in training students for the identified job-related competence.

The creation of an optimal learning environment: from a teacher-centred to student-centred approach

Knowledge transmission has long been regarded as a major function of higher education institutions. The higher education institution is then defined as an institution that exists to provide instruction through which knowledge is disseminated (Barr & Tagg, 1995; Jarvis, 2001). The traditional pedagogic approach, according to Chall (2000), was dominated by the teacher-centred method. This 'old' method was described as a passive lecture-discussion format where faculty talks and most students listen in a classroom setting (Barr & Tagg, 1995; Gauthier, 1995). This traditional pedagogic approach, which is characterised as 'didactic and directive' emphasising the recall of theoretical knowledge, is increasingly recognised as an ineffective way to enhance student learning (Bligh, 1995; Mann & Kaufman, 1995). Since the 1960s, there has been a paradigm shift from teaching to learning (Barr & Tagg, 1995; DeZure, 2000; Jarvis, 2002).

In redirecting the educational focus to learning, the student-centred pedagogy is believed to be creating a learning environment where students would be more actively involved and their individual differences would be accommodated (Gautheir, 1995). Attempts have been made by many researchers to delineate such a learning environment in order to optimise and enhance student learning. Norman (1993) states that the optimal learning environment should provide a high intensity of interaction, set goals and procedures, a feeling of challenge, and a sense of direct engagement with a work-related experience that would motivate learning. Bonwell (1991) suggested five major elements of an active learning environment as follows:

- student are involved in more than listening;
- less emphasis is placed on transmitting information and more on developing students' skills;
- students are involved in higher-order thinking (analysis, synthesis, evaluation);
- students are engaged in activities (e.g. reading, discussing, writing); and
- greater emphasis is placed on students' exploration of their own attitudes and values.

Accordingly, the pedagogic approach would have to involve students in doing things and thinking about what they are doing so as to promote active learning.

Jarvis (2001) proposed his model of the experiential learning process as the one realising 'real learning'. He defines learning as 'the process of individuals constructing and transforming experience into knowledge, skills, attitudes, values, beliefs, emotions and the senses' (p. 63). The core of this model is the 'transformation' or 'change' that has to take place in order to make 'real learning' possible. For Jarvis, an experience of a student in a classroom setting presented with a lecture may not result in learning if the student simply memorises the knowledge or reflects on it. In order to allow learning of knowledge and development of skills, Jarvis suggests the creation of a situation of 'disjuncture' under which students identify what is unknown and what information, skills, etc. are needed in order to solve the problem; they then need to pursue and discover the required information and it is through this process that they 'learn'.

The advocates of the optimal learning environment to enhance active learning share a common thread – learning by doing. Learning by doing has the implication that the curriculum must move from a teacher-centred to a student-centred approach. Problem-based learning represents one of the student-centred approaches that has increasingly been adopted.

A student-centred pedagogy: problem-based learning (PBL)

Problem-based learning as a type of student-centred approach originated in the field of medical education in the 1960s. It is basically a model with tutors guiding students to work on problems, which in turn drive learning (Sibley, 1989; Barrows & Tamblyn, 1980). Students are engaged in an experience in which the process of learning unfolds through the application of knowledge and skills to the solution of 'real' problems in the context of 'real' practice (Bligh, 1995; Fenwick, 1998).

Students assume responsibility for their own learning in the process of problem solving. A problem from a real-life context is presented to the students and they are required to discuss among themselves, reason about the problem, apply prior knowledge and identify the issues that they need to learn in order to solve the problem (Barrows & Tamblyn, 1980). The problem then serves as a focus to initiate learning through acquisition, application and integration of knowledge. In this process, learning outcomes of developing problem-solving skills, teamwork skills, self-learning skills and information searching skills could be achieved (Barrows, 1996).

The self-directed learning shapes the individual patterns of study and, through this process, students could develop skills that are required in the merchandising profession.

Reform of the course of Fashion Merchandising

The course of Fashion Merchandising was first introduced to the undergraduate programme in 1995. The curriculum was basically structured according to the functional areas of fashion merchandising. Concepts and theories were built into each area; and transmitted to the students by traditional formal lectures supplemented with case studies. This teaching method is characterised by so-called surface learning – that students are simply required to recall pieces of theories or show surface understanding to handle the assessment requirement. Students find it difficult to apply concepts to real-life situations and they are found lack motivation in learning. In addition to this negative student-learning attitude, employers in the fashion business have also complained that graduates are particularly weak in communicating ideas, negotiation, self-motivation, identifying information sources and solving problems.

To address the deficiencies of students and cope with the ever-changing and globalised environment of the fashion business, the course of Fashion Merchandising was restructured based on the PBL concept in 2000. In collaboration with the practitioners in the merchandising field, problem cases – each related to certain knowledge areas – were developed and incorporated into the new PBL-oriented course. As shown in Table 1, the course was restructured in such a way that the lectures and tutorials were built around each of the identified knowledge areas.

Cycle	Knowledge area	Lecture	Tutorial	Problem case
1	Planning and Product development	3 sessions	3 sessions	1
2	Sourcing	3 sessions	4 sessions	2
3	Quality and Export	4 sessions	4 sessions	3

Table 1 Course structure of Fashion Merchandising
Note: each lecture and tutorial session lasts for two hours

The new course pedagogy was not structured in a pure form of PBL. Instead, it is a hybrid PBL version, combining both traditional lecturing and PBL pedagogic methods. This is because of the fact that the course is only a part of the whole programme adopting the PBL approach. Time and resources available for students were limited and they imposed constraints in implementation. Therefore traditional lecturing, that has the advantage in supplying information in a timed manner, was the best option. The new course contained three tutorial cycles, each of which had three to four two-hour tutorial sessions. In the tutorial sessions, students work on a problem case (a total of three problem cases running in three tutorial cycles). In the first tutorial session of each cycle, students discussed the problem case and identified learning issues that were important for solving the problems. After this session, students were required to search for relevant information and knowledge (based on the identified learning issues) from various sources (e.g. lecture, library, interview). Students shared the information and knowledge in the second tutorial, during which they might generate further learning issues. In such cases, they repeated the process for the third tutorial session. With the obtained information and knowledge, they analysed the problem and then presented the solution in the last tutorial. Concurrently, lectures with predetermined content were conducted and they served as one of the sources of knowledge.

The course was so constructed to obtain the efficiency in knowledge dissemination by traditional pedagogic method and learning outcomes anticipated from PBL.

Methodology: evaluation of the PBL-oriented course

To evaluate the new course, both quantitative and qualitative methods were pursued to determine perceptions of student learning at the completion of the course. The use of these methods achieves coverage as well as depth. The evaluation was carried out in two phases. In the first phase, a questionnaire survey was conducted with 25 students of the 2001 class (80% of the total) and in the second phase, interviews were conducted with 17 students of the 2003 class (50% of the total).

Findings: questionnaire survey

In phase 1, a questionnaire containing four open-ended questions was designed to investigate the students' learning experience in terms of their attitudes towards the PBL-oriented course, the perceived learning outcomes and their comments on the course structure and delivery.

Attitudes towards PBL pedagogy

The 25 respondents were students of the undergraduate programme completing the course of Fashion Merchandising in 2001. Of the respondents, 92% had a positive attitude towards the PBL-oriented course and they preferred this learning approach over the traditional lecturing format. Table 2 shows the reasons for their preferences for PBL pedagogy.

Reasons	Percentage of total
Interesting	48
Skill improvement	40
Real-life	40
Practical	36
Active involvement	32
Self-directed learning	20
Enhance memory	12
Others	8

Table 2 Reasons for students of the 2001 class preferring PBL pedagogy

The new PBL pedagogy was considered to be more interesting than the traditional lecturing approach. The students had a feeling of real-life situations, resembling the actual working environment of merchandising personnel. Through the active involvement in solving problems, they found the importance of knowledge and they were able to apply the knowledge learned. They considered the problem as a stimulator initiating learning. They had full control over the process and learning was self-directed. They felt that they learned more because, rather than the short-term memorisation, they sought more information outside the traditional curriculum and they were able to understand the concepts and theories. They also learned different types of skills in the learning process such as analysis, presentation and information searching.

Perceived learning outcomes
Skills

All the respondents stated that they had improvement in skills, which included teamwork, problem solving, information searching, analysis, and communication and presentation. 60% of them developed skills in working with group members. They learned to communicate and contribute in the group. Almost half of them learned to solve problems. 32% of the students developed information searching skills in the process. They learned how and where to source information. It is through the search and analysis of information that they solve the problems. Some of them stated that their presentation skills had improved because they were required to share their ideas and information with others in the tutorial sessions.

Knowledge

Most of them claimed that they gained merchandising-related knowledge and knew more about the working life of a merchandiser. In addition to what was conveyed in the lectures and in the problem cases, some of them acquired other knowledge, for example in technical fields and in the field of international business. They acknowledged prior knowledge and sought new information as part of the knowledge gained in the course. This somehow reflects the capability of the students to self-learn and also recognition of the complex nature of knowledge that is not confined to any discipline.

Attitude

In comparison with skills and knowledge, students were relatively less attentive to the attitude aspect. Four of the respondents did not recognise any improvement of attitude from the course. However, a significant portion of them (48%) admitted that they had developed a sense of responsibility when working with their group members. 40% of them claimed that they learned self-management. They had to organise well and manage their time properly so as to facilitate group work and contribute to the group's success. A few of them learned to share with others politely and develop an enthusiastic attitude. From these findings, the attitudes that had developed among the students are found to be strongly related to the group work required in the course.

Views on course structure and delivery

Students were asked to comment on the new course in terms of structure and delivery. Students did not hold consistent views on the timing of lectures and tutorials. While 32% of them mentioned that they considered the time for tutorials to be not enough, 28% of them stated that the time was enough for both lectures and tutorials. 12% of them felt that there was not enough time for preparation before the next tutorials. The preparation involves information search, discussion among members and development of presentation materials. A week's time was considered to be too tight for completing these tasks. Two of them proposed adding more lectures because the problem cases made them feel inadequate in knowledge. Another two preferred smaller groups because they thought that it would be easier to work with fewer people and they would have more chance of expressing their ideas. Their comments were taken into account in modifying the course for the following academic year.

Findings: interview

Based on the experiences and comments of the students, some major changes were made to restructure the course of Fashion Merchandising. Firstly, in view of the tight schedule of one course to cover all the content areas, the course of Fashion Merchandising was split into two separate courses: (1) Principles of Fashion Merchandising and (2) Managerial Fashion Merchandising. Secondly, each of the courses is composed of lectures and tutorials structured on two problem cases. More time is allowed for lectures, tutorials and student preparation.

Interviews were conducted with students after completing the course of Managerial Fashion Merchandising. These aimed to investigate in depth students' perceptions of the course and their learning experiences. Unlike the questionnaire survey conducted in the first phase, this evaluation focused on seeking meaning behind people's words.

A self-directed learning in group

The interview data confirm the findings of the previous survey. Students considered the PBL approach to be an interesting way of learning. In comparison with traditional lecturing, PBL is less boring and has given them a lively and relaxed learning environment. In this environment, they were confronted with cases that resembled the real working life. The problem cases, as claimed by many students, initiated self-directed learning. Some of them considered this to be a very difficult time because they were provided with inadequate information from the ill-structured problem cases. Many of them felt confused and lost direction in the initial stage. In this aspect, some of them appreciated the efficiency of traditional lecturing in conveying the 'necessary' knowledge in a relatively short period of time.

Many students showed great desire to have control over their learning. To solve the problem, they had to participate in the process of searching for information, discussing, sharing information and preparing presentations. Many of them claimed that they had devoted too much time to the course by meeting members every week and working even on weekends. They claimed that this led to a heavy workload. However, this level of involvement or commitment gave them satisfaction and they appreciated the meaningful outcomes in such self-directed learning. In addition, many of them pointed out that the PBL approach allowed them to learn in greater depth and breadth. They learned more because they were required to search for information that was not only confined to the predetermined knowledge areas. They were required to share the knowledge with others and apply the knowledge in the problem cases. As such, they need to have a thorough understanding of the knowledge. The demand for understanding has in turn led to longer-term memorisation that could not be achieved through surface learning in the traditional lecturing format.

Students were required to work in groups in the PBL-oriented course and their performance was inevitably affected by their group members. The data showed both positive and negative views about group work and its effects. On the one hand, students may have less control over their own performance because their group mates may affect their performance. On the other hand, many of them have a stronger sense of responsibility because individual performance and contribution would significantly affect the overall group performance and thus their peer's grade.

A deep learning of knowledge

Most of the interviewed students claimed that they had gained in knowledge. They could identify, through solving problem cases, the knowledge they were lacking. To understand, communicate and solve the problems, they would have to clarify terms, seek knowledge that may not have been covered adequately in the lecture material, study the knowledge in detail and apply the knowledge to a real-life situation (as stipulated by the problem case). Through this process, they learned knowledge that covered key areas in merchandising as well as related knowledge that was outside the course plan. The students demonstrated initiative in seeking and integrating previous and new knowledge. A student's response provides a typical example:

> I have really gained the knowledge. For example, I learned L/C from the lecture and I know how it is used and applied in the real-life situation.
> From this course, I can understand the work of a merchandiser and I think I can apply what I have learned in my future career. It's useful.

In addition to the gain in knowledge, all the interviewed students claimed that they had improved their skills and attitudes. Most of them mentioned the enhancement of presentation and teamwork skills. They needed to present twice for every tutorial cycle and there was question and answer session after each presentation. In preparing for the presentation, they would have to ensure that they understood the material and included comprehensive supporting evidence so as to meet the challenge they may face in the Q&A session. This has thus driven them to enhance their skills and confidence in presentation. The following represents a typical response:

> Before every presentation I would rehearse several times and ask peers for comments. Therefore, my presentation skill is improved and I am now brave enough to present in front of the class.

Students worked in groups throughout the tutorial cycles. They learned how to coordinate group work, communicate their ideas with team members, accept others' ideas and in some cases, they learned how to compromise. They also learned to be more considerate and to handle disputes in the group. They were motivated to be more aggressive and responsive. Many of them claimed that the pedagogic approach created a kind of competition among groups and interdependency within groups.

They also developed skills of information searching and problem solving. A response from an interviewed student demonstrates their learning of research skills:

> In the past, I did not go to the library searching for information. After
> studying this course, I have got used to seek information in the library.
> Now I can make use of the facilities in the library quite skilfully.

In solving the problem, students learned how to identify problems, analyse logically, organise information systematically and formulate solutions from a holistic viewpoint. The training has significantly improved their technique in organisation and analysis. This can be revealed from a student's experience as follows:

> In the past, I solve problem by intuition. Now I know the procedure in
> solving problem. I can really do it by considering different factors
> before coming up with the solution.

Real learning through PBL pedagogy

The findings on students' perceptions and learning experiences give an overall picture of the PBL implementation in the undergraduate course from the students' perspective. It exemplifies that PBL provides an optimal learning environment for 'real learning'.

Real working situation

The problems resemble the real working situation of a merchandiser. The simulated working environment engages students with experiences of merchandising. The activity of solving problems, based on Jarvis's 'experiential learning process' framework, leads them to transform their experiences into knowledge and skills. The students thus stated that they had 'really learned something'. The problem cases are considered to be so real that enthusiasm is developed. The importance of learning knowledge and skills is also recognised through this process.

Self-directed learning

Students initiate the learning themselves. They identify learning issues and decide what to learn. They control the means and pace of learning according to their own preferences. On the one hand, individual differences are accommodated and, on the other hand, this sense of control over learning fosters a 'meaningful' learning environment in which students develop their learning habits. In this self-directed learning atmosphere, they 'learn more and deeper'.

Knowledge integration

In a real-life situation, problems are seldom confined to a single knowledge area. Integration of knowledge and skills is required to solve problems. In the PBL learning environment, students are free to acquire knowledge from different disciplines. The problem provides a focus for students learning to integrate prior and new knowledge.

Transferable skills

PBL provides excellent conditions for the development of skills. The group work, knowledge sharing and problem solving process provide a natural setting for the development of skills that are important for their future career. In the PBL-oriented course, students are put in an environment of conflicting human interaction, complicated work relations, excessive but incomplete information and competition. Through active participation, students learn the skills to deal with others, present ideas, search for information and more important, to analyse and evaluate by higher order thinking.

Conclusion

The research findings show a positive attitude of the students towards the use of PBL pedagogy in the course of Fashion Merchandising. The new curriculum has motivated and enthused students to acquire knowledge. The concept of self-directed learning remains as the focal point initialising a chain of learning experiences. With the incorporation of work-related elements in the problem cases, students experience the real-life dynamics that exist in their future working environment. The development of students' skills is found to be the most rewarding outcome. The encouraging results of the course evaluation suggests the success of using the student-centred pedagogic approach in equipping students at university level with the appropriate knowledge and skills for merchandising work. However, the course evaluation is based on the student's perception, which tends to be rather subjective in relation to their feelings about their learning experiences. Although it represents an important aspect in evaluating a student-centred course, data on student's performance in terms of knowledge and skills may provide additional information from another aspect judging its effectiveness in achieving the target goals. Future study on PBL pedagogy may collect information of students' performance in two other aspects: (1) their course performance in the school; (2) their performance in the real working environment. This may thus require quantitative evaluation of the students' knowledge and skills through structured assessment methods such as observation or test. As for the evaluation of their performance in the working environment, this could probably be done after their graduation. This may require a tracer study of those graduates working in the merchandising field and collaboration with their employers. The data may provide useful information for the improvement of the course structure and pedagogy in meeting the needs of the students as well as the industry.

References

Barr, R.B. & Tagg, J. (1995), 'From teaching to learning – a new paradigm for undergraduate education', *Change Magazine*, 27, 6, pp. 12-25

Barrows, H.S. & Tamblyn, R.B. (1980), *Problem-based Learning: An Approach to Medical Education* (New York: Springer)

Barrows, H.S. (1996) 'Problem-based learning in medicine and beyond: A brief overview', in Wilkerson, L. & Gijselaers, W.H. (eds.) Bringing Problem-Based Learning to Higher Education: Theory and Practice (San Francisco: Jossey-Bass Publishers

Bligh, J. (1995), 'Problem-based learning in medicine: an introduction', *Postgraduate Medical Journal*, 71, 836, pp. 323-32

Bonwell, C.C. (1991), *Active Learning: Creating Excitement in the Classroom* (Washington, D.C.: School of Education and Human Development, George Washington University)

Boud, D. & Feletti, G. (eds.) (1991), *The Challenge of Problem-based Learning* (London: Kogan Page)

Bridges, E.M. & Hallinger, P. (1991), 'Problem-based learning: a promising approach for preparing educational administrators', *UCEA Review*, 32, 3, pp. 3-8

Chall, J.S. (2000), *The Academic Achievement Challenge: What Really Works in the Classroom?* (New York: The Guilford Press)

80

DeZure, D. (2000), *Conclusions, in DeZure, D. (ed.) Learning From Change: Landmarks in Teaching and Learning in Higher Education from Change Magazine,* 1969-1999 (Sterling, Virginia: Stylus Publishing)

Fair, N.B., Hamilton, J.A. & Norum, P.S. (1990), 'Textile knowledge for merchandising professionals: significance for pedagogy in clothing and textiles', *Clothing and Textiles Research Journal,* 8, 2, pp. 29-37

Fenwick, T. (1998), 'Boldly solving the world: a critical analysis of problem-based learning as a method of professional education', *Studies in the Education of Adults,* 30, 1, pp. 53-66

Garde, A.R., Kane, C.D. & Mahajan, S.D. (2000), 'Improving textile education', *Textile Asia,* 31, 3, pp. 50-52

Gauthier, H. (1995), 'The challenge is change: moving from teaching to learning', *Ohio Board of Regents Newsletter,* 1, 3

Greenwood, K.M. (1981), 'Directions in the development of fashion merchandising curriculum in the 80s', *Proceedings of the Association of College Professors of Textiles and Clothing,* pp. 201-211

Hari P. K., Goyal R. & Behera B.K. (2002), 'Web based interactive learning for textile designing', *Proceedings of International Textile Clothing and Design Conference: Magic World of Textiles,* 6-9 October, pp.604-608

Jarvis, P (2001), *Universities and Corporate Universities: The Higher Learning Industry in Global Society* (London: Kogan Page)

Jarvis, P. (2002), 'Teaching styles and teaching methods', in Jarvis, P. (ed) *The Theory and Practice of Teaching* (London: Kogan Page)

Kellomaki, K. & Pesoneu, J. (1996), 'New aspects of textiles and clothing design education: Freija-network project of the Nordic countries', *Proceedings of 30th Symposium on Novelties in Textiles,* 12-14 June, pp. 131-133

Kelly, B. (1980) 'Comparison of perceptions of employment executives and retail educators on areas of competence for mid-management retailers', Summary, *Proceedings of the Association of College Professors of Textiles and Clothing*, pp. 101-102

Ladchumananandasivam, R. & de Medeiroos, J.I. (1999), 'Textile education in Brazil', *Textile Magazine*, 28, 3, pp. 6-

Lam, J.K.C. & McCabe, D. (1997), 'Development of inter-active web tutorial teaching for textile students', *Papers presented at the 78th World Conference of the Textile Institute in Association with the 5th Textile Symposium of SEVE and SEPVE*, 24-26 May, pp. 433-44

Mann, K.V. & Kaufman, D.M. (1995), 'A response to the ACME-TRI report: the Dalhousie problem-based learning curriculum', *Medical Education*, 29, 1, pp. 13-21

Mock, G.N. (2000), 'The development of textile higher education in the United States', *Textile Chemist and Colorist & American Dyestuff Reporter*, 32, 8, pp. 72-7

Morrison, J. (2004), 'Where now for problem based learning?' *The Lancet*, 363, p. 17

Norman, D. (1993), *Things That Make Us Smart: Defending Human Attributes in the Age of the Machine Reading* (Reading, MA: Addison-Wesley

Norman, G.R. & Schmidt, H.G. (1992), 'The psychological basis of problem-based learning: a review of the evidence', *Academic Medicine*, 67, pp. 557-565

Priest, A. (1995) 'Education and training for co-operation in the fashion world of tomorrow – the challenges', *Papers Presented at the World Conference*, 21-24 May, pp. 394-406

Richards, A.F. (1996), 'Textile education in the United Kingdom', *Abstracts of Lectures and Posters: Symposium on Novelties in Textiles*, 12-14 June, pp. 24-2

Rusu, C. (1996) 'Academic textile education, training and research development in Romania', *Papers presented at the 77th World Conference of the Textile Institute (Niches in the World of Textiles)*, 22-24 May, pp. 113-125

82

Schmidt, H.G., Norman, G.R. & Boshuizen, H.P.A. (1990), 'A cognitive perspective on medical expertise: theory and implications', *Academic Medicine*, 65, pp. 611-62

Sibley, J.C. (1989), 'Toward an emphasis on problem solving in teaching and learning: the McMaster experience', in Schmidt, H.G. et al. (eds.) *New Directions for Medical Education: Problem-based Learning and Community-oriented Medical Education*, pp. 145-157 (New York: Springer-Verlag

Taylor, G. (1999), 'Product development tuition in the problem-based learning mode', *Papers presented at the World Conference* (Textile Industry: Winning Strategies for the New Millennium), 10-13 February, pp. 293-298

Vernon, D.T. (1995), 'Attitudes and opinions of faculty tutors about problem-based learning', *Academic Medicine*, 70, 3, pp. 216-223

Williams, A. & Williams, P.J. (1997), 'Problem-based learning: an appropriate methodology for technology education', *Research in Science & Technology Education*, 15, 1, pp. 91-103

Biographical note

Betty Li Shu Wan. The author was previously the Assistant Professor in the Institute of Textiles and Clothing, Hong Kong Polytechnic University. She received her Associateship in textile technology (marketing) from Hong Kong Polytechnic University and has wide working experience in the textile and clothing field. Her academic life began when she pursued her MPhil study at Hong Kong Polytechnic University.

She has two streams of research interest. One is in the area of textile education and the other in fashion merchandising. On the one hand, she conducted research in determining the relationship between the textile industry and the education sector in Southeast Asia. Her doctoral thesis was an investigation into the institutional identity of China's textile education under the changing economic environment. On the other hand, she got involved in the project 'Sourcing information and manual for merchandisers of Hong Kong textiles and clothing industry' through which a widely recognised information manual was published. Her enthusiasm in continuously improving the training of fashion merchandisers has initiated her interest in pursuing research in the area of problem-based learning (PBL) pedagogy. She was the chief investigator of the project 'Revitalising the course of fashion merchandising through PBL pedagogy' from which this paper was developed. She also continues her teaching in the Clothing Industry Training Authority and the Hong Kong Polytechnic University on a part-time basis.

Faculty of Education, the University of Hong Kong is the place where she obtained her PhD and also the place where she began to develop her interest in child education. While she is the visiting lecturer with a teaching specialism in Fashion Merchandising, now she is also the programme director of a child learning centre.p6 The new PBL pedagogy was considered to be interesting and less bored than the traditional lecturing approach.

Construction of a clothing production system designed to satisfy individual requirements using computers

Yoshiko Sujino and Kazuko Ikeda
Bunka Women's University, Tokyo, Japan

Introduction

Until now, clothing-related education in universities has merely served to support the performance and perceptions of personnel training in the clothing industry, by imparting advanced theories on pattern making and overall competence in sewing techniques suited to practical items and materials. The object has been to thoroughly impart garment creation styles aimed at specialised professions, such as designers, patterners, graders, MDs, and fashion advisors, in line with the realities of production and distribution by Japan's apparel industry. This education used to function effectively for the specialised apparel system that has pertained until now. Today, however, there is a higher level of satisfaction of material needs, as well as changing preferences and physical attributes associated with diversifying consumer needs and aging. The system of education could hardly be said to be responding adequately to these changes. Thus, due to the inevitable need to improve the satisfaction levels of individual consumers, we are required to shift to a style of garment creation that involves the consumers themselves, quite unlike the conventional system of mass production. We also need to train human resources personnel, who will be equipped with integrated skills in clothing design in response to this shift. Meanwhile, the rapid advance of IT technology has made information networking a reality, and has dramatically expanded the work volume attainable by a single personal computer. This has created an environment in which these changes will be possible.

In this research, therefore, our aim is to create a university curriculum based on a total system of clothing manufacture that integrates CG, three-dimensional measuring instruments, apparel CAD, pattern printers, industrial sewing machines, and others, by connecting them

86

with computers. In this way, we will create an environment in which it will be possible to totally simulate and physically experience systems of apparel product manufacture, from planning and design to production.

Background initiatives for consumer participation in product planning

The current consumer awareness of ready-made products is that they are satisfied with materials, prices, sewing, ease of management and other such factors, but not with the limited designs and colour variation, limited availability of sizes, limited variety of products, and so on. The clothing industry is also trying to find proposals for new systems, to address the fact that conventional apparel systems no longer function amid this diversification of consumer needs. These systems include SPA (manufacturing retail) and order-made systems, as well as manufacturing systems such as BTO (Build To Order) and SCM (Supply Chain Management), and sales marketing such as one-to-one marketing and mobile marketing. In the retail trade, similarly, there are efforts such as in-store consumer-participation product design. Dissatisfaction with ready-made clothing has led to a rising interest in order-made systems and original garments. In a survey on student awareness of order-made systems (as shown in Figure 1), many respondents said they wished to purchase under order-made systems, with a support rate of 58%. But only 11% actually make purchases.

Figure 1 Support ratio and diffusion ratio of order-made apparel

As the figures suggest, there is considerable interest in order-made systems, with positive views that order-made systems can create designs to suit individual proportions and preferences, and moreover that the tailoring seems good. But on the other hand, doubts were also expressed: that prices are too high, there are too few garment types, and the stores are unknown. In tandem with efforts by the industry to seek proposals for user-friendly systems, the awareness of consumers also appears to be changing.

Initiatives for consumer participation in product planning, and the use of personal computers for the whole sequence from design to sewing, have already been proposed by many researchers and companies. But initiatives based on research never go beyond the stage of paradigm proposals, and have yet to reach the level of full implementation. At corporate level, similarly, these are merely seen as experiments, and in many cases are limited and small in scale. Given these changes in awareness, the apparel industry needs human resources personnel who understand product creation on a total level, as well as the conventional type of specialised personnel.

Meanwhile, education in this field also needs to shift to training human resources personnel who can respond to these changes. In fact, this proposal for a 'Clothing Production System Designed to Satisfy Individual Requirements' is not a completely new experiment, but is already being practised in individual classes in actual sites of education. Because these classes have been offered individually, however, the students attending them have not seen them as part of a coherent whole. It has been difficult for the students to grasp relationships and to gain a clear understanding of the overall picture. This time, therefore, we have concentrated on linking these together and allowing students to experience the entire production flow in a single item of clothing.

The clothing production system designed to satisfy individual requirements

The flowchart below outlines the concept of the 'Clothing Production System Designed to Satisfy Individual Requirements' being proposed here. The shaded parts are those that are already being developed in actual classes, individually or partially. What we are trying to propose this time is that these subjects that are being developed individually should be linked together. Students should be assisted in understanding the system through simulated experience of the flow of apparel manufacturing and should finally acquire this as knowledge.

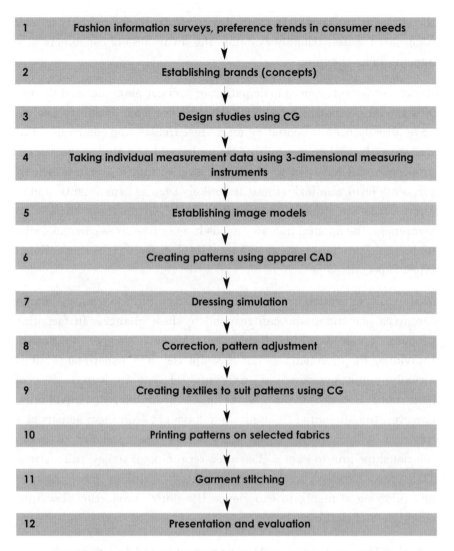

1	Fashion information surveys, preference trends in consumer needs
2	Establishing brands (concepts)
3	Design studies using CG
4	Taking individual measurement data using 3-dimensional measuring instruments
5	Establishing image models
6	Creating patterns using apparel CAD
7	Dressing simulation
8	Correction, pattern adjustment
9	Creating textiles to suit patterns using CG
10	Printing patterns on selected fabrics
11	Garment stitching
12	Presentation and evaluation

Figure 2 Conceptual flow of the Clothing Production System Designed to Satisfy Individual Requirements

Next, we will discuss concrete examples (mainly being developed in the 'Apparel Planning and Design' fourth-year special course in line with this system) and the problems encountered.

1 Fashion information surveys, preference trends in consumer needs

In terms of fashion information, the course focuses on thoroughly analysing fashion collections, street fashion, materials and other information via documentary surveys, fixed-point observation, in-store surveys, questionnaire surveys, etc. and grasping fashion trends, while at the same time accurately ascertaining preference trends in consumer needs. The aim is for students to understand how to accurately grasp types of information in line with the flow of information.

As facilities for researching information inside the university, we have a 'Fashion Resource Center', a 'Library' and a 'Museum'. We also give guidance on making use of these facilities.

The Fashion Resource Center consists of three sections, namely a Textile Archive Room, a Costume Archive Room and an Audiovisual Materials Room. Of these, the Textile Archive Room and the Audiovisual Materials Room are freely available for use by students. The Textile Archive Room includes a system for searching actual materials from a database. These, and card-sized samples of materials for textile proposals, are divided by colour and by material in a colour box, and are used for making maps. The Audiovisual Materials Room contains 80,000 designs, mainly from the Paris collections. It offers a system for searching by year and by brand, and can also provide printouts. This provides an environment for searching design sources from video images, as well as studies going all the way to map manufacture (Figure 3).

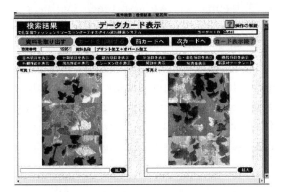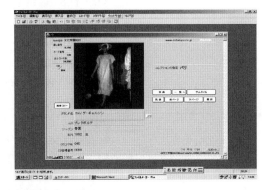

Figure 3 Fashion Resource Center (textiles and designers search page)

The Library contains most of the latest fashion publications – the core of fashion information – from both Japan and overseas. It even allows access to expensive fashion journals such as Promostyl. Back numbers of past fashion magazines are also available in its collections, with 120 overseas titles and 140 Japanese ones. Daily newspapers are of course provided, as well as latest issues and back copies of all the specialist newspapers.

All of these are available on open shelves for students to handle and view freely. They can also be photocopied. Students are encouraged to use these materials. For students who tend to fall into very narrow ranges of interest, an environment providing design information from the past gives them the knowledge with which to enhance their designs. The designs we have used as case examples are based on the Courrege and Cardin miniskirts from the 1960s and 70s. Valuable information was provided by photographs from the Audiovisual Materials Room, together with photographs and work examples from collections of fashion magazine back numbers provided by the Library.

The Fashion Museum has many outstanding exhibits from past and present, east and west. It has frequently attracted the attention of television, newspapers and other media. Exhibitions are held four times a year and admission is free to students. Since information gathering using actual documentary materials is highly effective, we offer guided tours, as well as explaining the content. The exhibits have also been converted to digital media and compiled in a database. This can be perused through graphic images on the Internet and terminals in the museum, and we encourage such use.

With the recent advance of IT technology, we also teach methods of searching and gathering information over the Internet, through practical use. We develop this to actual application through the net environment of our PC classrooms and practical study on image synthesis from net information. Recently, in particular, information on consumer needs via overseas collections is becoming increasingly important. There is a lot of information on the net, and we encourage students to search this information, as well as gathering information on the street and in stores.

Besides gathering information from documentary sources, we also apply methods of gathering and analysing information through surveys. Groups of students are given themes and use personal computers to statistically process questionnaire surveys. Using personal computers in groups, they learn how to prepare, print, distribute and collect questionnaire papers in accordance with their themes, then input, aggregate, tabulate and examine the data, compile reports and fulfil other processes via practical study.

This content is also taken up partially in the Clothing Formation classes in Years 1 and 2, and is then further developed in 'Fashion Information Surveys', a specialist course in Year 3 (Figure 4).

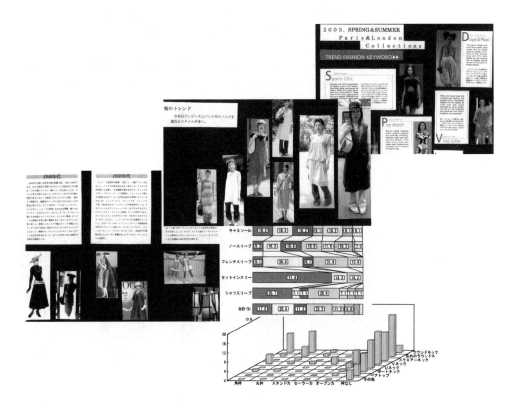

Figure 4 Students' works (collections, street, history, questionnaires)

2 Establishing brands (concepts)

In brand planning, we establish brands from the results of comprehensive analysis of consumer needs and preference trends, and clearly indicate the brand concepts. Having done this, we also analyse the trends of rival brands, making use of information on fashion trends as shown earlier (targets, product characteristics, life scenes, quality, sales territory, etc.), and clarify the brand's positioning. We bring this all together to create planning proposals aimed at the following season, including themes, design points, product composition, price range, sales point development methods, and so on. We then hold thorough discussion on the indicated planning proposals, and study and correct them, before producing final planning proposals and test-producing samples.

3 Studies using CG design

Plenty of time is taken to draw up proposed brand designs for the following season, using CG as an effective tool. This is because of the need to make visual presentations of design variations and coordinates, as well as the designs that form the core of the season.

In the preparation of design drawings, our teaching focuses on the ability to express the three-dimensionality, material texture and colour of designs in a more visual way (Figure 5).

Figure 5 Development of design variations

4 Taking individual measurement data using three-dimensional measuring instruments

Taking individual measurement data is an indispensable part of garment manufacture. The tape measure has long been used as an instrument to achieve this. Today, however, methods have changed greatly, and this university set out to develop new techniques at a very early stage. As well as Martin's Anthropometric Instruments approved under JIS standards, we have also installed a Silhouetter System (automatic body imager) and a Moiré Topography Camera, besides the sliding gauge developed mainly by this university. We are using these in our classes and research. In addition to these, our predecessors at the university have been involved in developing three-dimensional measuring instruments (today's leading-edge technology) from the outset. We currently have two of these, including one for research. The other one (a Body Line Scanner) was introduced last year, and soon will be freely available for use by a large number of students. The time taken for a whole body measurement is about ten seconds at 2.5mm pitch. Also, as well as measuring the human body, it can also take cross-section images and multiple-section images. We are currently constructing a system that will be able to continuously measure individual human bodies and extract individual physical information from the gathered measurements, instantaneously and at any time. Meanwhile, plans are now under way to enable physiques to be classified from the gathered individual human body measurement data, master patterns to be made for target customers and these to be used in the development of grading rules, etc. The construction of these systems in future will surely be useful to developing real body-based dummies and industrial dummies. It should also help to improve garment design capability, allowing pattern makers to ascertain the physical attributes of target customers with a view to increasing customer satisfaction (Figure 6).

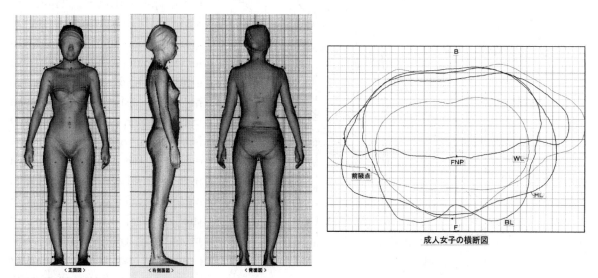

Figure 6 Human body measurement using three-dimensional measuring instruments

94

5 Establishing image models

Here, to make the brand image more visual, the focus is on establishing brand image models. Specifically, this means extracting three-dimensional measurement data and understanding physical attributes in more visual terms.

6 Creating patterns using apparel CAD

Patterns are made from the proposed design drawings using apparel CAD. The patterns are matched to the assumed brand targets and incorporate the human body measurement data and physical attributes of the image models. Alternatively, patterns produced through three-dimensional cutting are scanned into a personal computer and turned into digital data. This conversion to digital data means that '(8) Correction, pattern adjustment' can be addressed more quickly, which in turn helps us to proceed to CG pattern printing.

Practical CAD tuition in pattern-making involves creating two-dimensional patterns and learning three-dimensional cutting techniques in Years 1 and 2. Having assimilated these, in Year 3, patterns of basic items like blouses, skirts and tailored jackets are made from processing chest dart volumes based on the manipulation of prototype patterns. Then, in Year 4, tuition moves on to manipulation methods for high-level pattern-making and grading and verification of patterns. Mastering pattern manipulation using apparel CAD is vital in order to meet the demand for training pattern makers and graders equipped with direct competitive ability in the apparel industry. In all probability, this will have to be gradually expanded to earlier years as well in future (Figure 7).

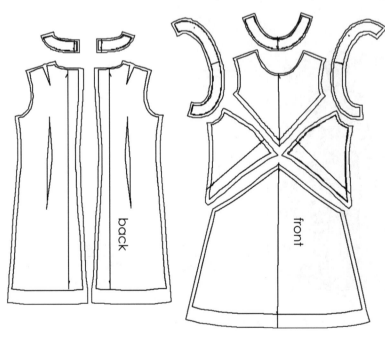

Figure 7 Dressing Simulation

7 Dressing simulation

Using the industrial patterns created in (6) and the physical data in (4), as well as fabric data, the patterns are dressed on image models in three-dimensional image depictions. The visually expressed design image and film are appraised, then corrected. The software used can simulate three-dimensional shapes by inputting data on the pattern, body and fabric characteristics. The dressed state reproduces a realistic silhouette incorporating fabric characteristics and makes it possible to confirm design in quite considerable detail. A major characteristic is that changes in design lines on the dressing simulation are automatically reflected in the pattern. Another is that the three-dimensional depiction can be viewed as transparent, with colour distribution, in cross-section, etc., making it possible to visualize the space between the person and the garment. The software used in dressing simulation is a field in which development is ongoing. Although in some aspects incomplete, this software has a good relationship with patterns. It is only partly being used by this university, but development is expected to proceed with further use from now on (Figure 8).

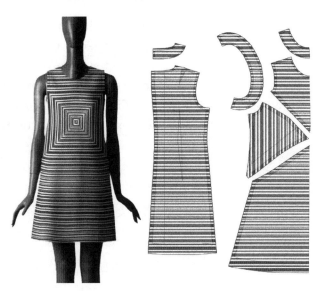

Figure 8 Dressing simulation (synthetic)

8 Correction, pattern adjustment

Being able to adjust patterns directly based on the results of the dressing simulation in (7) is extremely significant in terms of work efficiency. By combining devices that have, until now, been used individually into a single system, this system can be used organically in both industry and education. Unfortunately, we still have problems with the flow of processes from CAD data in (6) to pattern printing in (10). Although individual components are already complete and being used efficiently, files are not yet completely interchangeable, and this makes it difficult to proceed smoothly. We are currently engaged in joint improvement efforts together with CG and CAD software suppliers. Technically, this is not such difficult work, but we are trying to find a way of alerting the industry to the aspect of 'forward investment' by education in a procedure which is not commercially profitable. Luckily, this is also now regarded as important by the apparel industry, and improvements are expected in the near future.

9 Creating textiles to suit patterns using CG

The textile, including the original design proposal, the size and arrangement of the pattern and the colour, are formed as a composite whole, directly over the finally amended industrial pattern. This is then appraised.

The technique is simple, and each student can freely create original patterns using CG. Enabling students who understand patterns and garment structure to consider printed patterns means that they have more opportunities to create their own unique patterns for clothes. This is a different development to patterns made from square fabric shapes. For example, the pattern shown in Figure 9 is a simple striped pattern.

Figure 9 Using CG to create a pattern (striped)

By drawing this on top of the pattern, the student is able to create a pattern (incorporating the darts volume on the chest) that would not be possible by cutting from square fabric.

If the students are able to create fabric patterns individually, originally and freely, this gives them the great satisfaction of being able to express their ideas and creativity. It also makes it easy for them to visually perceive and understand the structure of garments in an enjoyable way. As such, the learning effects can be said to be very significant.

10 Printing patterns on selected fabrics

Fabric needs to be treated before and after fabric printing. Here, we provide fabrics that have first been pre-treated externally, print on them with inkjet printers and then treat them again. Conventionally, technology for printing patterns on fabric used to involve equipment aimed at mass production. The machinery was large and often not suitable for operation by non-professionals. Even when the machinery was smaller, it tended to be used individually by different sectors and was difficult to use unmodified in educational sites. Now, thanks to increasing compactness and lower prices, this is indeed possible. Pre-treatment and post-treatment of fabric is indispensable to reproducing the vividness and stability of colour. This proves very troublesome when you actually try to do it. However, 'polymer dying' technology, which does not require pre- and post-treatment, has now been developed, and targets for commercialisation have emerged in the last year or so. This is technology that we would like to improve while making use of it (Figure 10).

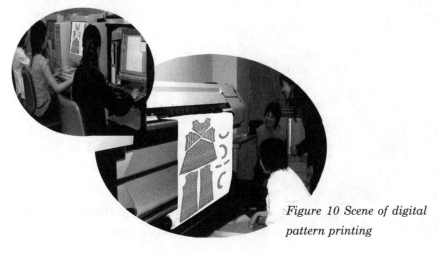

Figure 10 Scene of digital pattern printing

11 Garment stitching

In this process, we decide the sewing conditions and secondary materials, efficiently stitch actual garments based on sewing process analysis charts, dress them on the human body, study and appraise. We also produce sewing specifications at this time.

Efforts to teach garment stitching in sites of education are mainly a case of understanding through individual manufacturing. This is because, even in an era when people are sent to work in sites of mass production, learning about manufacturing through a single garment enables students to grasp the structure of clothing and its problems. This method is obviously indispensable to individual manufacturing and other attempts to meet diversifying consumer needs, as mentioned above. Of course, we also include knowledge and technology on sewing machines in mass production systems as a separate part of our curriculum. But besides this practical training in sewing manufacture by creating individual garments, we also recently introduced practical cutting and sewing with the use of mass production machinery and are now preparing to start operation in around November 2005. The training scene in Figure 11 shows equipment already being used in our institute's Bunka Fashion College.

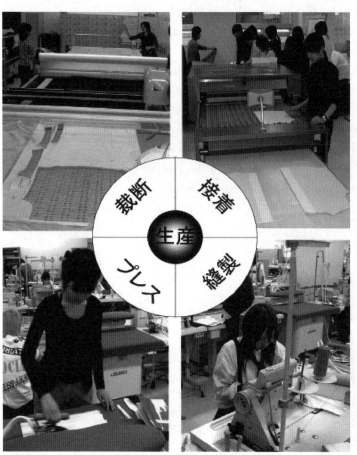

Figure 11 Scene of practical training in sewing manufacture

This new development will allow us to offer practical training in sewing techniques using CAM cutting, bonding and sewing machines similar to this existing equipment or at a newer, higher level.

12 Presentation and evaluation

In the above, we have described our processes designed to satisfy the purchasing inclinations of individual consumers in timely fashion. Firstly, the individual appraises and selects the preferred garment designs using virtual CG. Then, based on individual physique measurement data obtained from three-dimensional measuring instruments, we create a pattern using apparel CAD. Next, a material that suits individual preferences is chosen, the textile is appraised and confirmed through dressing simulation and the pattern is corrected. Finally, fabric is actually placed over the pattern, the pattern is printed and the cut fabric is stitched. Through this total process of clothing manufacture, the planning proposal is presented and evaluated. The ultimate objective of the teaching is to remind students of the importance of apparel product planning and to impart the ability to judge the value of a product.

Methods of presentation and evaluation in the curriculum involve setting up shops and booths at the university's cultural festival and elsewhere and holding exhibitions, making use of mannequins and fixtures. These efforts are effective.

Figure 12 (overleaf) outlines this flow, including the relationship between hardware and software. Although the system is not yet complete, we consider it possible to produce results by amending and improving while actually developing the system.

Summary

We have attempted to create a total process of garment manufacture using computers and to positively introduce and promote it in our curriculum as part of our practical tuition. As the culmination of this education, it has been introduced and firmly incorporated in classes such as practical learning in costume manufacturing and creation of apparel brand planning proposals for our 'fashion shows'. These are regarded as a special characteristic and tradition of this university, and the results have been well evaluated. We conclude that this is an effective tuition

100

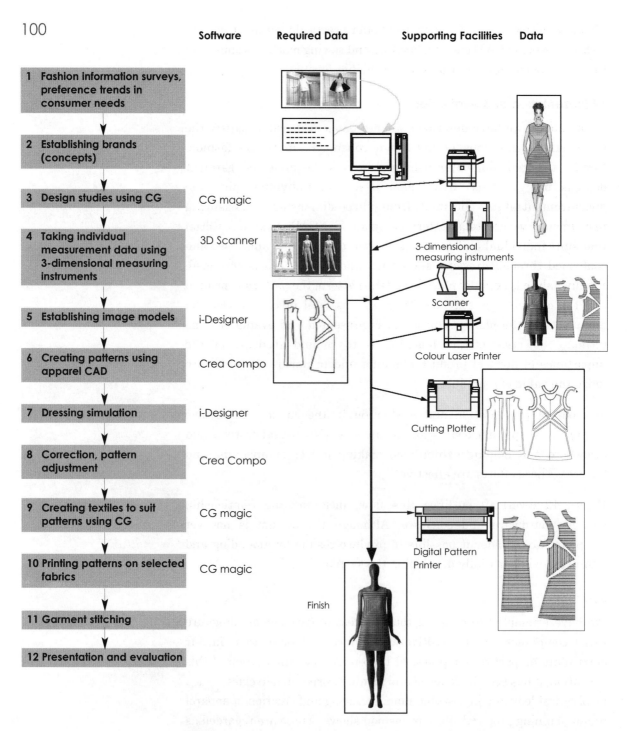

	Software	Required Data	Supporting Facilities	Data

1 Fashion information surveys, preference trends in consumer needs

2 Establishing brands (concepts)

3 Design studies using CG — CG magic

4 Taking individual measurement data using 3-dimensional measuring instruments — 3D Scanner — 3-dimensional measuring instruments

5 Establishing image models — i-Designer — Scanner

6 Creating patterns using apparel CAD — Crea Compo — Colour Laser Printer

7 Dressing simulation — i-Designer — Cutting Plotter

8 Correction, pattern adjustment — Crea Compo

9 Creating textiles to suit patterns using CG — CG magic — Digital Pattern Printer

10 Printing patterns on selected fabrics — CG magic

11 Garment stitching — Finish

12 Presentation and evaluation

Figure 12 Basic composition of the Clothing Production System Designed to Satisfy Individual Requirements

system that contributes to training 'total modelists', and leads to greater employment opportunities for them, as opposed to training aimed at specialised aspects of production processes in the apparel industry as it is now. Judging from the trend towards overseas transfers of production bases, the diversification of consumer preferences and demands for improvement to more efficient productivity, these 'total modelists' will be much sought after by the apparel industry in future. Finally, in terms of future directions for improving customer satisfaction, our target is to create a system that will facilitate and simulate the so-called 'on demand' method. Under this method, consumers will be able to use computer networks to choose their own desired design, materials and colours from global as well as Japanese brands in the comfort of their own homes, place orders together with physical data and size information and obtain the actual garment at a later date.

Tasks for the future

We are attempting to improve the 'Clothing Production System Designed to Satisfy Individual Requirements Using Computers' proposed above, while continuing to experiment with it. The system is not yet completely connected. The problems that hinder us at the present time can be summarised as follows:

- developing the personal computer environment
  (1 PC per student);
- removing differences in students' PC competence levels;
- quickly achieving data compatibility between software;
- developing a network environment capable of large-volume CG data;
- harmonising awareness and levels of teaching staff;
- simplifying fabric treatment methods.

In future, we aim to accumulate know-how on operation while taking steps to solve these problems.

Acknowledgements

We would like to thank Mr. Ando and Ms. Yamaguchi of Toray ACS, Inc., for their kind cooperation in providing documentary materials.

102

References

Kakio, M. (2002), *Future Prospects for Mail-order Trading* (Senken-Shibun Co., Ltd.)

Kamei, Kinoshita, Yagi & Yamada (2003), 'A product planning support system based on self-organised maps using indicators of sensibility and physical indicators', *Proceedings of the 5th Annual Conference of the Japan Society of Kansei Engineering*, October 2003

Okada, Takadera & Shimizu (2003), 'Creation of a variable human body model for individually tailored garment design', *Proceedings of the 5th Annual Conference of the Japan Society of Kansei Engineering*, October 2003

Sato, R. (2002), *Apparel Design for Customer Satisfaction* (Senken-Shibun Co., Ltd.)

Biographical Notes

Yoshiko Sujino. Yoshiko Sujino teaches in the Department of Fashion, Faculty of Home Economics, Bunka Women's University. Her main interests and research areas are fashion technology, fashion design, and pattern design theory. Yoshiko Sujino's publications include Fashion Technology, Technology Section III, Formal Section, Special Materials Section (co-author, Bunka Women's University Textbook Publishing Department, 2001).

Kazuko Ikeda. Kazuko Ikeda teaches in the Department of Fashion, Faculty of Home Economics, Bunka Women's University. Kazuko's special interests and resarch are in fashion technology, fashion design, and fashion information research. Her publications include Fashion Technology, Technology Section (co-author, Bunka Women's University Textbook Publishing Department, 2001).

The Department of Fashion Technology offers three special courses in the 3rd year, namely the Fashion Production and Marketing Course, the Creative Fashion Course, and the Textile & Apparel Science Course. Of these, the authors are in charge of the Fashion Production and Marketing Course. This Course offers practical education, a characteristic of this University since its inauguration. The authors teach subjects such as "Fashion Design", "Fashion Technology", and "Pattern Design Theory". Besides these, they also give guidance to 4th year students who organize an annual "Fashion Show" as the culmination of all this learning.

This "Fashion Show" will be held for the 20th time this year. This is a major event, attracting a total of around 9,000 visitors to 6-8 showings over the space of three days. The 20th Show will involve 220 students and about 30 members of teaching staff. For the students who are involved in putting on the Show, this not only provides motivation to learn about fashion, but also helps them to acquire high-level skills, improve their presentation ability, and gain a sense of achievement. In the past, we have hosted joint shows with partners from Germany, Britain, China, South Korea, and other countries, helping to raise the profile of this University.

All students undertake compulsory "graduation research", each setting individual themes on which a thesis is prepared. As a result of these, the students acquire advanced creative skills and theory, leading to an employment rate of between 70 and 80% in the apparel industry.

Bunka Women's University was founded in 1923, with the mission of "Playing a central role in the diffusion and growth of Japan's fashion culture, and producing human resources who will benefit Japan's fashion industry", and the objective of "Undertaking specialist education and research to this end".

The present field of specialty, in the Faculty of Fashion Science, is to develop advanced education in apparel creation and design in the Department of Fashion Technology, and to pursue general socio-economic, cultural and historical aspects of fashion in the Department of Fashion Sociology. In the Faculty of Art & Design, everyday implements, information and industrial crafts are designed and produced in the Department of Crafts and Design, while, in the Department of Environmental Design, the aim is to create designs and proposals for interiors, housing, architecture, and others as a means to comfortable home living.

Research facilities have been set up in the "Bunka Gakuen Costume Museum" (1979), the Research Institute of Fashion Information Science (now the Bunka Research Lab for General Study of Fashion) (1985), and the Textile Museum (now the Fashion Resource Center) (1994.